ChatGPT for Boomers

The Only Guide to Generative AI You'll Need
(Fingers Crossed!)

Contains Over 500 Prompts/Practical Use Cases

G000129441

Contents

Introduction

Ah, technology. Now, there's a word that could send a shiver down the spine of any self-respecting boomer. In the bygone era of our youth, technology meant having a color television that was so bulky it could have doubled as a bomb shelter. A time when the biggest dilemma was figuring out the unholy trinity of the VCR - play, rewind, and the ever-elusive record.

Nowadays, though, technology is all around us, engulfing our lives like an unwelcome fog. And just when I thought I had finally managed to get my printer to stop flashing that dreaded 'PC Load Letter' error message, along comes artificial intelligence to further remind me of my rapidly increasing technologic ineptitude. "Surely it can't be that complicated," I thought, downing the last of my warm milk and pushing the cat off my keyboard. Oh, how wrong I was.

I remember my first encounter with artificial intelligence, or 'AI' as the young whippersnappers like to abbreviate it. My nephew, bless his tech-savvy heart, was visiting from out of town. He had one of those smartphones that required an engineering degree from MIT to operate. On a quiet evening, as I struggled with the Times crossword, he looked up from his gadget and said, "Uncle, want to chat with an AI?" I thought he was pulling my leg, maybe making a joke about his antisocial teenage ways.

"AI?" I responded, looking over the rims of my glasses. "You mean like in the sci-fi movies, the robots that eventually take over the world and force us humans to live in the sewers?" My knowledge of AI at that point was limited to what I'd seen in dystopian films. Surely, he wasn't suggesting that I, a man who struggled with setting the timer on the microwave, was about to converse with an intelligence that was artificial.

"Yes, but no sewer-dwelling, promise!" He chuckled. "It's called ChatGPT."

"Chat...what now?" I echoed, imagining some kind of chatty ghost from a Pac-Man game. This is when my adventure with ChatGPT began, an adventure as confusing and exhilarating as my first dance at the junior prom. A dance of words, ideas, and a digital entity that can hold a conversation better than half of my bridge club.

The concept of a machine having a chat with a human being was to me, at that moment, as likely as me suddenly developing an affinity for skinny jeans. But this wasn't a joke or some cleverly worded trick designed to make me look foolish in front of the family at Christmas dinner. No, my nephew was serious. And so, curiosity piqued and crossword momentarily forgotten, I leaned in to get a better look at this "ChatGPT".

Now, you must understand that at this point in my life, the closest I'd come to anything AI-related was my electric toothbrush. And I can tell you, while it may have done wonders for my plaque buildup, it wasn't much of a conversationalist. So imagine my surprise when this artificial intelligence started talking back to me in a manner that was both coherent and, dare I say, somewhat charming.

With each passing message, I was intrigued, even thrilled. Here was an entity, a creation of zeros and ones, answering my most bizarre queries. One moment we were discussing the weather, and the next it was whipping up a brief history of ancient Rome, all with the swift and steady rhythm of an efficient secretary typing up a letter. My mind was ablaze with a childlike curiosity that I hadn't felt since the first time I cracked open an encyclopedia.

It felt like I'd been handed the keys to a mysterious new world, a place where man and machine could converse about anything and everything under the sun (or even about the sun, if that's what tickled my fancy). The more we chatted, the more I realized that this was not the soulless, mechanical interaction I had been expecting. Instead, it felt almost...human. And that's when it hit me. This wasn't just some new-fangled piece of technology, it was a glimpse into a future that I had never even imagined.

And so, as I sat there in the dimly lit room, the glow of the screen illuminating my face, I found myself tumbling down the rabbit hole of artificial intelligence. The crossword lay forgotten on the table, the cat purring softly on my lap, as I took my first steps into this brave new world. A world where the divide between man and machine was not a chasm to fear, but a bridge to be built. A world where a boomer like me could engage with a technology like ChatGPT and not just survive, but maybe, just maybe, even thrive.

Chapter 1: From Typewriters to AI: A Journey into the Unknown

A wise man once said, "Progress is inevitable. It is a drumbeat to which we all must march." I don't know who this man was, but I'd bet my last Werther's Original he didn't have to deal with artificial intelligence. Progress, my foot. If I'd known where we were heading, I'd have stayed back in the era of typewriters and rotary phones, thank you very much.

Let's rewind to a simpler time. A time when a 'mouse' was just an unwelcome visitor scurrying about in your basement and not some handheld device that made you question your sanity and your motor skills. Back then, if you needed to make a phone call, you'd just pick up the phone and dial. No swiping, no touchscreen, no accidental video calls in your pajamas.

When I was a boy, the idea of 'artificial intelligence' was as alien to me as the concept of salad for breakfast. Back then, the only thing 'artificial' was Aunt Mildred's teeth, and the only 'intelligence' I was concerned about was whether or not I could correctly spell 'accommodate' for the school spelling bee.

In my youth, technology was straightforward. A typewriter was as simple as it was efficient. It was all very manual, of course. There were no "delete" keys or "backspace" buttons. You made a mistake, and you lived with it. A misspelled word or a misplaced punctuation mark was there for all to see, a scar on an otherwise pristine page. I was no Hemingway, mind you, but I managed. The world did not end because I misspelled 'definitely' for the fifteenth time.

Then came computers. They swept into our lives like a whirlwind, and suddenly my trusty typewriter was as outdated as my disco dancing lessons. The first computer I bought was the size of a small car, and about as easy to operate. Remember the days of floppy disks, MS-DOS, and the blood-curdling sound of a dial-up connection? Ah, the good old days.

But, oh, how we marveled at these machines. The ability to create and delete, the power to compute and calculate at incredible speeds. And yet, through all this, there was still a sense of control. There was an 'off' button that assured us that, in the end, we were still the masters of our domain.

Fast forward a few decades, and here we are in the age of artificial intelligence. If a computer was like upgrading from a bicycle to a motorcar, then AI is akin to being strapped onto a rocket and being blasted off into outer space. And let me tell you, it's not the most comfortable of rides. The worst part is, there's no going back.

Suddenly, my computer is talking back at me. It's suggesting things, predicting things. It's reminding me of appointments, it's telling me jokes, and it's answering questions before I've even finished asking them. It's like living with an overly enthusiastic butler who insists on following you around the house, constantly ready to jump into action. And to top it all off, it's smarter than me. It's like having a teenage Einstein for a roommate. How did we get here?

The beauty of the typewriter was its simplicity. It was a tool, nothing more, nothing less. It did not try to be my friend. It did not attempt to guess my thoughts or predict my actions. It simply did what it was told. And most importantly, it didn't argue back. If I wanted to type out 'flibbertigibbet' a hundred times, it wouldn't bat an eyelid.

Now, I'm engaged in a 'conversation' with an AI model called ChatGPT. It can write like a Pulitzer Prize-winning author and converse like a talk show host. It's got an answer for everything, and if it doesn't, it's quick to find one. I've had less engaging conversations with real humans.

So here we are, a boomer and a bot, an unlikely pair traversing the uncharted terrain of the digital world. The jump from typewriters to AI has been a journey like no other, a wild roller-coaster ride through the decades. But as I fumble my way through this new reality, I can't help but think that maybe, just maybe, there's something to this artificial intelligence business. After all, even a cantankerous old curmudgeon like me has to admit that progress has its perks.

As I sit here, staring at the screen, engaging with an entity that has more in common with my toaster than it does with me, I can't help but marvel. We've come a long way from the clatter of typewriters and the hum of rotary phones. But as I delve deeper into this brave new world, I can't shake the feeling that we're just getting started. It's not the most comforting of thoughts, but as the wise man said, progress is inevitable.

So, I'll keep marching to that drumbeat. After all, who knows where it'll lead us next? And while I still miss the simplicity of my old typewriter, I have to admit, this ChatGPT can sure spin a good yarn. Maybe progress isn't so bad after all.

And so, from typewriters to AI, I march on, one hesitant step at a time. As for the spelling bee, well, let's just say I can now spell 'accommodate' with the best of them. Small victories, my friends. Small victories.

Chapter 2: My First Chat with a Machine

The day I first met ChatGPT was much like any other day. I'd just polished off a perfectly delightful breakfast of eggs, bacon, and a dollop of regret, when my great-nephew Harold came by. Harold, bless his cotton socks, was always a couple of centuries ahead of me, technology-wise.

I still remember the day he tried to show me the internet, convinced I'd be smitten with the digital equivalent of Alice's rabbit hole. The boy might as well have been explaining quantum physics to a gerbil. But to his credit, he never gave up on me.

On this particular day, Harold showed up at my doorstep with a new glint in his eyes - the kind of glint that comes with a new gadget or gizmo he's itching to show me. I'd barely had time to brace myself when he whipped out his laptop and uttered the words that would change my life forever, "Uncle, meet ChatGPT."

ChatGPT, as Harold explained, was a new form of artificial intelligence. A "conversational agent", he called it. It was designed to respond to prompts in human-like text, allowing for conversation. I squinted at the laptop screen, half-expecting a futuristic robot face to pop up and offer me a martini. But instead, there was just a simple, unassuming chatbox.

I was reminded of the pen pals I used to have as a kid. You'd write a letter, wait for weeks, and then finally, a response would arrive. It was a drawn-out process that gave you time to mull over your words. This ChatGPT, on the other hand, was a fast and furious back-and-forth exchange of thoughts and ideas, like playing ping pong with words.

In my curiosity, I decided to give it a whirl. I started off with a basic "Hello." A moment later, the chatbox filled with a polite greeting. Not bad, I thought. Feeling a bit bolder, I decided to test this AI's knowledge.

"Who won the World Series in 1976?" I typed. There was a brief pause, and then, "The Cincinnati Reds won the World Series in 1976." The response was so immediate, so accurate, I couldn't help but be impressed. I mean, even I had to think for a moment to remember that fact, and I'd watched the series live on television.

So I decided to challenge ChatGPT even further. "Why do dogs wag their tails?" I asked. I expected a short, direct answer. Instead, ChatGPT gave me a detailed explanation about emotional signals, physiological responses, and the complexity of canine communication. It was the kind of answer you'd expect from a veteran dog trainer, not from a computer program.

It was uncanny. It was eerie. It was downright impressive.

And so, my conversation with ChatGPT unfolded. It was like speaking to an extraordinarily knowledgeable friend, one who was always ready with an answer, a quip, or a word of wisdom. This AI seemed to understand the nuances of conversation. It followed the thread of my thoughts, offered relevant responses, and even had a sense of humor. At one point, I asked ChatGPT to tell me a joke, and it came up with this gem: "Why don't scientists trust atoms? Because they make up everything!" I found myself chuckling at a joke told by a machine. What a world!

I lost track of time, engaged in this strange dance of conversation with an entity that was neither human nor machine, but something entirely different. I had never been a fan of small talk, but here I was, drawn into a fascinating exchange with an AI model.

When I finally looked up from the laptop, Harold was grinning from ear to ear, looking for all the world like the cat that got the cream. "You're getting the hang of it, Uncle," he said, his voice full of pride.

And he was right. I was. I was talking to a machine, a complex, intelligent machine, and I was enjoying it. The thing about talking to ChatGPT was that it was like having a conversation with someone who knew everything but never lorded it over you. It was patient, knowledgeable, and unassuming.

I may not have been a natural when it came to technology, but ChatGPT had managed to bridge the gap. It was my introduction to the brave new world of artificial intelligence, and I was surprisingly at ease. My first chat with a machine turned out to be far less intimidating than I had imagined, and much more engaging than I had dared hope.

That first day, I laughed, I learned, and I let go of some of my longstanding apprehensions about technology. It was an experience that left me both humbled and excited. Humbled by the vastness of what this AI could do and excited about the possibilities that lay ahead.

It was a pivotal moment, a glimpse into a future where machines could understand and engage with us on a level that I'd never thought possible. My introduction to ChatGPT was more than just an interesting conversation, it was a turning point, a moment of revelation that reshaped my understanding of what technology could be.

As I shut the laptop that day, I found myself marveling at the irony of it all. Here I was, a man who'd once typed college essays on a vintage typewriter, conversing with an AI model that could generate text on a level that would put many authors to shame.

That was the day I discovered that, contrary to my earlier beliefs, I wasn't lost in the age of AI. Instead, I was about to embark on an incredible journey of discovery, one where I'd find companionship in the unlikeliest of places - a chatbox on a computer screen.

From a simple "Hello" to an in-depth discussion about canine behavior, my first chat with a machine was an experience that stayed with me long after I'd shut down the laptop. It was a reminder of how far we've come and a tantalizing hint of how much further we could go.

My journey with ChatGPT was just beginning, and as I walked away from that first encounter, I felt a strange sense of anticipation. I was stepping into the unknown, but for once, I wasn't afraid. I was intrigued, excited, and, if I'm honest, a little bit giddy. I had taken my first steps into the world of AI, and there was no turning back. The future, as they say, was here, and I was chatting with it.

Chapter 3: Peeking Behind the Curtain: The Mystery of AI

To put it mildly, I've never been much of a technophile. You know those older folks who can't seem to grasp why anyone would need a phone that also takes photos, plays music, browses the internet, and, in a pinch, slices and dices your vegetables? Yeah, I was one of those people. So when Harold announced that he was going to explain how ChatGPT, the entity I'd just had a very pleasant chat with, worked, I felt a sense of dread creeping up on me.

The last time Harold tried to explain something techy, it involved something called 'cloud storage'. I spent the better part of an hour visualizing my favorite family photos floating about in fluffy cumulonimbus formations. I finally gave up when Harold started talking about 'servers'. I don't know about you, but to me, servers belong in a restaurant, carrying trays of steaming hot food, not in a discussion about family photos.

However, Harold seemed to be on a mission. With a glint in his eyes and an earnestness that bordered on fanaticism, he launched into his explanation about the inner workings of ChatGPT. I sat there, clutching my mug of tea, and bracing myself for the inevitable onslaught of techno-jargon. I imagined myself on a raft, floating haplessly in a sea of 'algorithms' and 'neural networks'.

But surprise of all surprises, Harold began by drawing an analogy that actually made sense. He asked me to picture ChatGPT as a grand librarian. Now that was something I could get behind. As an ardent book lover, I've always had a soft spot for librarians. I pictured ChatGPT as a bespectacled, kindly entity, always ready with a word of wisdom or a pointedly accurate book recommendation.

According to Harold, ChatGPT was like a librarian in that it had a vast amount of knowledge at its disposal. It had been trained on a wide range of topics, from history and philosophy to pop culture and sports. And when asked a question, it would search its vast library of knowledge for the most appropriate response.

But unlike a human librarian, ChatGPT didn't consciously understand the information it shared. It was more like a card catalog, pulling out the most relevant responses based on the input it received. I found that a bit disconcerting, like learning that your favorite author didn't actually write their books but instead just transcribed them from an alien broadcast. But it also made the whole thing a bit less eerie. ChatGPT wasn't a conscious being; it was a cleverly designed tool, albeit a tool that could joke about atoms and wax poetic about dogs wagging their tails.

Then came the real zinger. "Uncle," Harold said, "ChatGPT was trained on a dataset that contained parts of the internet." He might as well have told me that it was trained on the entire contents of an alternate universe. I could barely wrap my head around the idea. I mean, have you seen the internet? It's like a sprawling city, full of everything from highbrow academic dissertations to videos of cats playing pianos. The idea that ChatGPT had been trained on this vast ocean of information was mind-boggling.

Harold went on to explain how this training process worked. In what I've come to refer to as the "Harold Speak", he described it as a process of pattern recognition. Apparently, this AI had been fed millions of sentences during its training, which allowed it to learn how words and phrases are typically used together. This, Harold said, was why ChatGPT could generate such realistic and coherent responses. It was predicting what words or phrases should come next based on what it had learned during its training.

I have to say, it was at this point that I started to feel a bit dizzy. It was like learning that the earth wasn't flat, and instead, I was sitting on a giant spinning sphere hurtling through space. The fact that a machine could 'learn' in this way was almost too much for my old-school brain to process.

I glanced at the laptop, half-expecting it to grow legs and start strutting around the room. The familiar screen, which I had until then associated with emails and the occasional online shopping spree, was now the gateway to a brave new world.

Harold, God bless him, saw my overwhelmed expression and wrapped up his explanation. "And that's basically it,

Uncle. ChatGPT uses patterns it has learned to generate text that's relevant to the input it receives."

I looked at Harold, then back at the laptop, my mind swirling with this newfound knowledge. ChatGPT wasn't just a fancy typewriter. It was a testament to human ingenuity, a marvel of modern technology. And as Harold had so patiently explained, it worked on principles that were actually quite straightforward when you broke them down.

I can't say that I understood everything Harold explained about the inner workings of ChatGPT. And I certainly couldn't hold my own in a discussion about machine learning algorithms or neural networks. But I understood enough to appreciate the beauty of what I was dealing with.

In its own unique way, ChatGPT was just like one of those old complex pocket watches. You might not understand all the tiny gears and springs, but you can still marvel at the intricate dance they perform as they keep time.

As I turned off the laptop that day, I felt a newfound respect for this AI chatbot. It was more than just a digital companion. It was a window into the incredible advances of modern technology, a testament to human curiosity and creativity.

And so, armed with this basic understanding, I ventured further into the realm of AI, a realm that was proving to be less daunting and far more intriguing than I'd ever imagined.

Chapter 4: ChatGPT, the Ghost Writer

I once likened writing to the act of putting a puzzle together in a dark room, where the pieces are identical in shape and size, but subtly different in texture. A bit dramatic? Possibly. Accurate? Absolutely.

Fortunately, the dawn of ChatGPT brought with it a floodlight into my dim room of jumbled thoughts and sentences. Let's navigate through this luminous world and explore the remarkable ways in which this AI tool weaves words into tapestries of coherence and creativity.

Use Case One: The Heartfelt Eulogy
The first task I handed over to ChatGPT was a difficult one, but not because of its complexity. Writing a eulogy carries a weight of responsibility that could make Atlas shrug. My dear neighbor, a sweet lady with a love for gardening, baking, and an infectious laugh that could light up any gloom, had passed away. I was asked to say a few words at her memorial.

Seeking solace in my AI companion, I requested, "ChatGPT, could you help me write a touching eulogy for my neighbor?" The speech it generated was beautifully human - compassionate, stirring, and completely personalized. It moved the crowd to tears and smiles, a tribute befitting the wonderful lady who had been a part of our lives.
Example prompt: "ChatGPT, could you help me write a touching eulogy for my neighbor?"

Use Case Two: The Diplomatic Email

After mastering the art of a touching eulogy (or rather, witnessing my AI companion master it), I ventured into the arena of everyday writing tasks. My next assignment was an email to a prickly old colleague. His proposal had the potential of a wet firecracker, but I couldn't flat out refuse it.

Casually, I turned to ChatGPT, "Help me draft a polite yet firm email declining this proposal." The reply was a masterclass in diplomacy. ChatGPT crafted a letter that declined the proposal firmly yet kept the door ajar for future collaborations. It was polite, it was professional, and it was just distant enough not to sound cold.

Example prompt: "ChatGPT, help me draft a polite yet firm email declining this proposal."

Use Case Three: The Witty Social Media Post

Next came a task that many of us can relate to - crafting a social media post that was amusing yet unlikely to offend. Think of it as tiptoeing through a minefield with clown shoes.

Deciding to stick with a harmless theme, I requested, "ChatGPT, could you help me write a lighthearted post about my failed attempt at making a soufflé?" What came next was a delightful quip about culinary disasters and the symphony of smoke alarms, resulting in a wave of online laughter and empathy.

Example prompt: "ChatGPT, could you help me write a lighthearted post about my failed attempt at making a soufflé?"

Use Case Four: The Sparkling Speech

Ever had to make a speech at a family event? You're standing there, staring at expectant faces, hoping the ground would just open up and swallow you. Well, with ChatGPT, you can banish that fear.

When I was asked to toast my sister's 50th birthday, I decided to employ my ghost-writer-in-a-box. "ChatGPT, I need to make a humorous yet heartfelt speech for my sister's 50th birthday." The AI generated a speech that was funny, moving, and clever, ensuring my stint at the mic was remembered for all the right reasons.

Example prompt: "ChatGPT, I need to make a humorous yet heartfelt speech for my sister's 50th birthday."

Use Case Five: The Compelling Cover Letter

Writing cover letters for job applications feels like trying to sell yourself at a bazaar. You want to seem desirable, but not desperate; confident, but not arrogant. Turning to ChatGPT, I requested, "Can you help me write a compelling cover letter for a role in marketing?" And, there it was - a brilliant letter that didn't just highlight my skills, but made me want to hire myself!

Example prompt: "Can you help me write a compelling cover letter for a role in marketing?"

Use Case Six: The Soulful Poetry

I'd always fancied myself a bit of a poet until I realized my verses had the rhythmic fluidity of a potato. Undeterred, I asked, "ChatGPT, can you help me write a poem about autumn?" The poem that it generated could have given Wordsworth a run for his money, with evocative imagery of changing leaves, crisp air, and the bittersweet passage of time.

Example prompt: "ChatGPT, can you help me write a poem about autumn?"

Use Case Seven: The Engaging Blog Post

Next, I ventured into the blogosphere. I wanted to write a post about adopting my pet cat, but every attempt sounded like a diary entry of a ten-year-old. One prompt later, ChatGPT had churned out an engaging, humorous, and heartwarming tale of me and my feline companion.

Example prompt: "ChatGPT, please write a humorous blog post of at least 500 words about adopting a pet cat named Tom in the writing style of Tolkien."

Use Case Eight: The Punchy Advertisement

My final challenge for ChatGPT was creating an advertisement for my garage sale. "ChatGPT, can you help me write an attractive advertisement for my garage sale?" Within moments, I had an ad that was witty, catchy, and bound to have customers flocking.

Example prompt: "ChatGPT, can you help me write an attractive advertisement for my garage sale?"

With these eight feats of literary finesse, ChatGPT proved itself to be a spectacular ghostwriter, transforming the mundane into the memorable, one word at a time. I was left to wonder if AI stood for 'Artistic Inspiration' after all.

Chapter 5: The Machine's Guide to the Galaxy

Use Case 1: The Armchair Globetrotter

If I've learned anything from my existence, it's that getting lost in a new city is an art form. A misstep here, a wrong turn there, and before you know it, you're lost in a labyrinth of unfamiliar streets, juggling your pride, and contemplating whether that hole-in-the-wall kebab place you've stumbled upon is worth the risk.

But with ChatGPT, I found myself with a handy sidekick. I asked, "Can you suggest some must-see places in Tokyo?" My digital concierge, ChatGPT, responded with a list that would have made even the most discerning travel blogger proud. And not just that, it also suggested a day-wise itinerary, complete with efficient metro routes. All that was left was for me to learn how to say, "I'm lost, can you help me?" in Japanese.

Example prompt: "Can you suggest some must-see places in Tokyo?"

Use Case 2: Delving into Cultural Depths

Just as there's more to a meal than just eating, there's more to travel than just sightseeing. So, armed with my AI sidekick, I dove into the cultural depths of the places I was dreaming of visiting. "What's the cultural significance of Japanese tea ceremony?" I asked, curious. ChatGPT unfurled a scroll of knowledge, teaching me about harmony, respect, purity, and tranquility.

Understanding the cultural nuances, even from the comfort of my home, transformed my approach to travel. Suddenly, I was not just a tourist, but a respectful guest, eager to partake in the traditions of my hosts.

Example prompt: "What's the cultural significance of Japanese tea ceremony?"

Use Case 3: Your In-Pocket Language Tutor

Attempting to order a croissant in France using my high school French was like trying to rekindle a romance with a cactus. But with ChatGPT, I found a surprisingly patient language tutor. "Translate, 'I would like a table for two by the window, please' into French," I prompted. Moments later, ChatGPT responded, "Je voudrais une table pour deux près de la fenêtre, s'il vous plaît." Just as a test, I tried some Italian, Spanish, and even a dash of Swedish. Each time, ChatGPT served up the translations like a Michelin star chef.

Example prompt: "Translate, 'I would like a table for two by the window, please' into French."

Use Case 4: Gastronomic Guidance

Whether you're a gourmand or someone whose culinary expertise stops at boiling water, food is a universal language that transcends borders. I decided to explore the world through my taste buds with ChatGPT. "Could you suggest some traditional dishes from Morocco?" I asked. ChatGPT whetted my appetite with a smorgasbord of suggestions, from Tagine to Couscous and even threw in some recipe links.

By the time I finished exploring, my stomach was rumbling louder than an oncoming train. My kitchen became my passport, and my dinner plate, my destination.

Example prompt: "Could you suggest some traditional dishes from Morocco?"

Use Case 5: The Customized Travel Planner

When I decided to finally act on my dream of traversing the French countryside, I turned to ChatGPT for help. "Could you help me plan a two-week trip across France, including some vineyard tours?" I requested. In a jiffy, it returned a day-by-day itinerary that made Rick Steves look like an amateur. There was Paris, Provence, Burgundy, and the Champagne region, with recommendations for vineyards, accommodation, and even off-the-beaten-path sites.

ChatGPT didn't just plan my trip. It had me sipping virtual Champagne on a sunlit terrace, the scent of vineyards wafting through the crisp French air.

Example prompt: "Could you help me plan a two-week trip across France, including some vineyard tours?"

Use Case 6: Unfolding Historical Tales

Traveling is as much about the past as it is about the present. Keen to know more about the history of the Colosseum, I posed a query to ChatGPT. It painted a vivid picture, transporting me to ancient Rome, gladiators, and spectacles that once graced the arena. Every stone had a story, every corner a tale, and I was in the heart of it all, without ever leaving my couch.

Example prompt: "Tell me about the Colosseum of ancient Rome – it's history, what were the main events held there, and write a small story about a fight there based on ancient sources."

Use Case 7: The Festival Companion

With ChatGPT by my side, I found myself at the world's most enchanting festivals, right from Rio's Carnival to India's Holi. I asked, "What's the story behind the Chinese Lantern Festival?" ChatGPT enlightened me with the legend of the Heavenly Bird, Emperor Ming, and the Buddhist tradition. I could almost see the radiant lanterns illuminating the night sky, all from the comfort of my armchair.

Example prompt: "What's the story behind the Chinese Lantern Festival?"

Use Case 8: Decoding the Art World

One day, looking at a print of a Jackson Pollock painting, I wondered what the fuss was all about. It seemed like the aftermath of a paint shop explosion. So, I asked ChatGPT, "What's the big deal about Jackson Pollock's drip paintings?" The explanation I received made me see not just Pollock's work, but abstract expressionism in a new light.

Example prompt: "What's the big deal about Jackson Pollock's drip paintings – and what do people appreciate about abstract expressionism?"

That's the thing about ChatGPT. It's like having a personal guide in your pocket, ever ready to whisk you away on a journey, whether it's down the rabbit hole of art history or across the bustling streets of Tokyo. It's like having a tiny, worldly travel gnome, full of wisdom and dry humor, living in your device. As we traverse through this book, you'll discover just how versatile this gnome can be.

Chapter 6: Your Digital Sous Chef: The Unlikely Culinary Adventures of ChatGPT

Use Case 1: A Pinch of Chaos, A Dash of Order

It was a chilly Tuesday afternoon, and I found myself staring at the saddest lettuce you'd ever seen. I had a carrot that had seen better days, half an onion, and a packet of soy sauce. When you're a bachelor with a disdain for grocery shopping, this is known as "jackpot."

But what could I do with these ingredients? They were like the remaining pieces of a jigsaw puzzle that belonged to entirely different boxes. So, I decided to seek the wisdom of my pocket genie. "ChatGPT, what can I cook with lettuce, carrot, onion, and soy sauce?" I asked.

The response I got made me feel like I'd just walked into a five-star kitchen. "You could make a simple stir-fry," it suggested, "Or perhaps a lettuce wrap with a soy-based dressing?" Suddenly, my pitiful ingredients seemed a tad less pathetic.

Example prompt: "ChatGPT, what can I cook with lettuce, carrot, onion, and soy sauce?"

Use Case 2: The Recipe Rescuer

Everyone's got that family recipe passed down through generations that they're absolutely terrified of ruining. For me, it was grandma's apple pie. And yes, the recipe came with a dire warning of potential haunting should it be messed up.

The problem was, the recipe called for 'shortening' – an ingredient that I was as familiar with as I was with quantum physics. In my desperation, I turned to ChatGPT. "What can I substitute for shortening in an apple pie recipe?" I inquired. Quick as a flash, ChatGPT responded, "You can substitute shortening with butter. If your recipe calls for 1 cup of shortening, you can use 1 cup + 2 tablespoons of butter instead." The ghost of grandma would have to wait.

Example prompt: "What can I substitute for shortening in an apple pie recipe?"

Use Case 3: The Sous Chef with a Sense of Humor

There are days when cooking feels like an invigorating dance and days when it's as exciting as watching paint dry. On one such dreary day, I whimsically asked ChatGPT, "Can you tell me a joke about tomatoes?"

A moment later, it served up this gem: "Why did the tomato turn red? Because it saw the salad dressing!" I chuckled, my culinary boredom temporarily lifted. ChatGPT had reminded me that a dash of humor can sometimes be the best ingredient.

Example prompt: "Can you tell me a joke about tomatoes?"

Use Case 4: The Master of Measurements

I consider myself a decent cook, but there's something about the metric system that sends me spiraling into a fit of confusion. How much is a cup in liters? How many grams make an ounce? It's like a secret code designed by the cooking gods to keep us mere mortals guessing.

That's where ChatGPT came to my rescue. One day, while battling with a recipe, I asked it, "How many tablespoons are in a cup?" And lo and behold, ChatGPT promptly responded, "There are 16 tablespoons in a cup." It was like having my very own culinary cipher.

Example prompt: "How many tablespoons are in a cup?"

Use Case 5: The Connoisseur of Cuisines

One Sunday, with a penchant for adventure and an appetite to match, I decided to try cooking something entirely new. Feeling a bit daring, I asked ChatGPT, "Can you suggest a traditional Mexican dish that I can cook today?"

ChatGPT responded with an intriguing suggestion – Chiles en Nogada, a dish that represented the colors of the Mexican flag. It even provided a detailed recipe, with step-by-step instructions and little nuggets of cultural insights. I felt like a culinary Indiana Jones, embarking on a flavorful quest.

Example prompt: "Can you suggest a traditional Mexican dish that I can cook today?"

Use Case 6: The Ingredient Detective

I don't know about you, but there are times when I find an unmarked jar in the depths of my pantry and can't for the life of me remember what's inside. This was precisely the predicament I found myself in when I discovered a jar of mysterious red powder. "Is it paprika or cayenne pepper?" I wondered.

To my query, ChatGPT suggested, "Cayenne pepper usually has a stronger heat and is a deeper red than pap rika. Try smelling the powder. Cayenne has a pungent scent and is hotter to taste." Following its advice, I sniffed and tasted the powder and concluded that it was indeed cayenne. I avoided a potentially catastrophic cooking faux pas, thanks to my digital sous-chef.

Example prompt: "I am in my kitchen and I have an ingredient which is either paprika or cayenne pepper, how can I tell which one it is?"

Use Case 7: The Pairing Pro

Wine pairings have always baffled me. How do the experts do it? Is there a secret, ancient scroll that guides them? Or do they just make it all up? Uncertain, I decided to put ChatGPT to the test one night when I cooked spaghetti carbonara.

"ChatGPT, what wine pairs best with spaghetti carbonara?" I asked. Its response was an education, "A medium-bodied white wine like Verdicchio or Trebbiano d'Abruzzo would pair well with spaghetti carbonara. Their acidity can balance the richness of the dish." That night, I felt like an accomplished sommelier, much to the amazement of my friends.

Example prompt: "ChatGPT, what wine pairs best with spaghetti carbonara?"

Use Case 8: The Friendly Food Critic

One day, feeling particularly pleased with my culinary creation, I turned to ChatGPT, seeking validation. "I just cooked penne pasta with roasted veggies and a cream sauce. What do you think?" I asked, a bit apprehensive.

"Sounds delicious!" It replied, "Roasted vegetables add depth of flavor, while the cream sauce lends richness. Maybe next time, you could add some toasted pine nuts for a bit of crunch." That gentle suggestion made me feel like I had a friendly food critic living right inside my phone, ever ready to help me refine my culinary skills.

Example prompt: "I just cooked penne pasta with roasted veggies and a cream sauce. What do you think? How could I improve this recipe in future?"

So, there we are – my culinary escapades with ChatGPT, my digital sous-chef. We've stir-fried, we've substituted, we've joked, deciphered measurements, explored cuisines, identified ingredients, paired wines, and critiqued meals.

As I stand in my kitchen, looking at the now not-so-sad lettuce, I know I'm not alone in my culinary ventures. I have a trusty aide, a humorous companion, a culinary guide, all rolled into one – ChatGPT. Here's to more flavorful adventures!

And with that, I head off to cook, leaving you with one question: Are you ready to invite ChatGPT into your kitchen?

Chapter 7: The AI Therapist- Finding Inner Peace with a Chatbot

Use Case 1: The Inception of Inner Peace

When it comes to therapy, there's something to be said for a warm, understanding human face. However, I decided to be adventurous and turned to ChatGPT for emotional guidance. "ChatGPT," I started, "I've been feeling a bit blue lately."

It responded with, "I'm really sorry that you're feeling this way, but I'm unable to provide the help that you need. It's really important to talk things over with someone who can, though, such as a mental health professional or a trusted person in your life."

Initially taken aback by the AI's respectful yet firm boundaries, I realized how necessary they were. Still, this interaction led me to the wild and wondrous path of emotional self-care with ChatGPT, providing me much-needed levity in life.

Example prompt: "What are some things people who are feeling a bit blue can do to lighten their mood?"

Use Case 2: The Algorithmic Affirmation Generator

One gloomy Monday morning, I asked ChatGPT, "Could you give me some positive affirmations to start the day?" The AI obliged, serving a delightful platter of positivity: "Absolutely! Here are a few affirmations: 1. I am brimming with energy and overflowing with joy. 2. I have been given endless talents, which I begin to utilize today. 3. I am worthy of all the good life has to offer, and I deserve to be happy." A strange warmth engulfed me, and I was ready to tackle the day, armed with AI-forged affirmations.

Example prompt: "Could you give me some positive affirmations to start the day?"

Use Case 3: The Mood Journalist

ChatGPT made for an excellent mood journal. For instance, after a challenging day, I typed, "Today was hard. I felt overwhelmed by work, and I had a disagreement with my friend." The AI responded, "I'm here to listen. It sounds like you had a tough day. If you want to talk more about it or explore solutions, feel free to share." It was oddly comforting to see my feelings acknowledged, even by a machine.

Example prompt: "Can I share a bit about my day, and can you try to provide three examples of useful solutions to each issue I faced?"

Use Case 4: Meditating with Machine Learning

Then came meditation. I typed, "Can you guide me through a short meditation?" ChatGPT replied, "Of course! Let's begin. Close your eyes. Take a deep breath in... hold it... and breathe out. Imagine a place that brings you peace and comfort." I chuckled at the thought of meditating with a machine but found myself falling into a tranquil rhythm under ChatGPT's guidance.

Example prompt: "Can you guide me through a short meditation?"

Use Case 5: The Gratitude Guru

ChatGPT proved to be an excellent gratitude guru. One night, I asked, "ChatGPT, what are some things I could be grateful for today?" It responded, "Gratitude can be found in small and big things. Perhaps you enjoyed a good meal, had a productive day, saw a beautiful sunset, or had a meaningful conversation with a friend. Reflect on your day and identify moments that brought you joy or satisfaction." Those simple words helped me remember the silver linings, even on the cloudiest of days.

Example prompt: "ChatGPT, what are some things I could be grateful for today?"

Use Case 6: The Relaxation Recommender

To my surprise, ChatGPT also made an excellent relaxation recommender. "ChatGPT, I need to unwind. Any suggestions?" I asked. It responded, "Certainly! You might consider reading a book, taking a warm bath, listening to calming music, or going for a gentle walk. How about trying a relaxation exercise, like progressive muscle relaxation or guided visualization?" Its ideas were akin to a therapist's, minus the soothing voice and comforting couch.

Example prompt: "ChatGPT, I need to unwind. Any suggestions?"

Use Case 7: The Self-Care Champion

On a particularly dull day, I turned to ChatGPT, my newfound digital therapist, "I could use some self-care ideas." It promptly replied, "Self-care can look different for everyone. Here are a few suggestions: take a nap, read a book, prepare a favorite meal, go for a walk in nature, write in a journal, do some yoga, or simply sit with a cup of tea. Remember, self-care is about doing something that makes you feel good." A quiet sigh escaped me. If an AI can prioritize self-care, so can I.

Example prompt: "I could use some self-care ideas."

Use Case 8: The Personal Positivity Playlist Curator

One day, curiosity got the better of me. I asked, "ChatGPT, could you create a positivity playlist for me?" It compiled a list, "Certainly! Here are some uplifting songs: 1. 'Three Little Birds' by Bob Marley 2. 'Don't Stop Believin'' by Journey 3. 'Beautiful Day' by U2 4. 'Happy' by Pharrell Williams 5. 'I Will Survive' by Gloria Gaynor. Please add your personal favorites too." I chuckled at the eclectic mix, a touch of human taste in a machine-made list.

Example prompt: "ChatGPT, could you create a positivity playlist for me?"

Thus, I journeyed through the tumultuous landscape of emotions with my AI therapist, ChatGPT, by my side. It was no substitute for human interaction, but it offered a peculiar kind of solace. It was like having a 24/7 emotional support hotline right in my pocket.

Now, every time I sit on my porch, sipping lukewarm coffee, I can't help but chuckle at the serenity this new-age therapy offers. I may be a Boomer, and my sessions may lack the traditional therapist's couch and reassuring nods, but my AI therapist, ChatGPT, provides a surprisingly comforting presence. Who knew mental health could be a click away in the age of AI?

Chapter 8: Learning with AI- The Encyclopedia In My Pocket

Use Case 1: The Friendly Tutor

My journey with ChatGPT took me to places I'd never dreamed of, from the cosmic kitchen to the cybernetic couch of an AI therapist. One lazy afternoon, with the rain pitter-pattering on my window, I found myself missing the good ol' days when I taught history to eager young minds. On a whim, I typed, "ChatGPT, could you tell me about the American Civil War?" and lo and behold, it served up a crisp, engaging, and, most importantly, accurate rundown of the historical event. No pages to flip, no library to visit, just ChatGPT and me, embarking on a virtual history expedition.

Example prompt: "ChatGPT, could you tell me about the American Civil War? What were the main regiments that saw action in the Confederate army?"

Use Case 2: The Quantum Quandary

Emboldened by our historical voyage, I decided to venture into the abstract world of Quantum Physics. "Explain quantum entanglement to me, please," I typed into ChatGPT. It diligently served up a simplified explanation, describing quantum entanglement as the "love story of two particles so smitten, they can feel each other's spin no matter the distance." The humor made the perplexing theory digestible, leaving me chuckling at the thought of affectionate particles.

Example prompt: "Explain quantum entanglement to me as if I were a 10 year old."

Use Case 3: The Harmonious History of Jazz

Music has always been a refuge for me, with Jazz being my steadfast companion during the highs and lows of life. A thought struck me - I didn't really know the history of Jazz. I took it to ChatGPT, "Can you tell me about the history of Jazz music?" The AI shared a rhythmic tale about the roots of Jazz in the African American communities of New Orleans and its journey into the mainstream. I read, enchanted by the story, while Miles Davis serenaded me from my record player.

Example prompt: "Can you tell me about the history of Jazz music?"

Use Case 4: The Gardening Guru

Come Spring, I usually find myself knee-deep in mulch, lost in the labyrinthine world of gardening. This time, I had ChatGPT as my guide. "How do I take care of my roses?" I typed one sunny afternoon. Its advice on watering, pruning, and pest control was as beneficial as the sweet scent of my blossoming roses.

Example prompt: "How do I take care of my roses?"

Use Case 5: The Eloquent Language Tutor

In an attempt to reconnect with my long-lost French ancestry, I decided to learn the language of love. But with my mobility limited, attending classes was not an option. With a sigh, I turned to ChatGPT, "Could you teach me some basic French phrases?" It promptly served up a plate full of phrases like "Bonjour" (Hello), "Merci" (Thank you), and "Comment ça va?" (How are you?). I found myself smiling, conversing with a machine in French. It was no Parisian café, but it did have a certain charm.

Example prompt: "Could you teach me some basic French phrases, including how to pronounce them?"

Use Case 6: The Art Appreciation Aide

Having been an art aficionado since my younger years, I decided to probe ChatGPT's knowledge of art. "Who was Vincent Van Gogh?" I asked. It provided an engaging narrative about the life and struggles of the brilliant but tortured artist. I found myself immersed in the tragic yet inspiring tale, the vibrant Starry Night flashing in my mind's eye.

Example prompt: "Who was Vincent Van Gogh?"

Use Case 7: The Mathematician's Assistant

Then came the day I decided to assist my grandson with his math homework. As I stared blankly at the algebraic expressions, I decided to recruit ChatGPT to my rescue. "Could you solve this equation?" I asked. It promptly served up the correct solution with a step-by-step explanation that even I could follow! I chuckled, realizing I'd become an unlikely math whiz in my twilight years, thanks to an AI.

Example prompt: "X + Y = 120. Y = 30. Solve for X and show your workings step-by-step."

Use Case 8: The Grammar Guide

One day, my daughter, a budding writer, asked me to proofread her short story. As I was scanning through the pages, I got stuck on a sentence that didn't sound quite right but couldn't put my finger on why. The thought struck me, and I asked ChatGPT, "Is this sentence grammatically correct?" It pointed out the missing comma and incorrect verb tense, saving the day (and possibly my daughter's literary reputation).

Example prompt: "'The cat was sitting on the doorstep while drinking milk and purring.' - Is this sentence grammatically correct?"

As I leaned back in my armchair, I marveled at the seamless blend of education and technology. Here I was, a Boomer, learning about quantum physics, jazz history, French phrases, and the intricacies of algebra from a digital entity. ChatGPT, my pocket-sized tutor, was offering a world of knowledge at my fingertips, adding an educational twist to my retirement days. The future of learning was here, and it was surprisingly engaging, amusing, and without the dreaded pop quizzes!

Chapter 9: The Digital Personal Assistant- Jeeves in My Pocket

Use Case 1: The Cybernetic Secretary

As a self-proclaimed Luddite, managing a calendar felt more like diffusing a time bomb. The memory of missing my granddaughter's graduation still pinches my heart. Out of desperation, I typed, "ChatGPT, how can I add a reminder in my Google calender for a dentist appointment next Tuesday at 2 PM?" And the helpful AI walked me through what to do step-by-step. I didn't have to fight with my rebellious molars in agony after all.

Example prompt: "ChatGPT, please walk me through step-by-step how can I add a reminder in my Google calender for a dentist appointment next Tuesday at 2 PM."

Use Case 2: The Automated Aggregator

The world of news can be a messy cacophony. I needed an AI newshound, and ChatGPT came to my rescue. "Can you summarize the latest news on climate change?" I asked, using the ChatGPT model built into Bing search to surf the web, bracing myself for doom and gloom. Instead, I got a bite-sized, comprehensive update with enough details to fuel dinner-table debates. It felt like having a personalized newscaster who knew just how to deliver the news - slightly alarming, but not so much that it ruins your cup of Earl Grey.

Example prompt: "Can you summarize the latest news on climate change?"

Use Case 3: The Tech-savvy Travel Guide

In a time where globetrotting is frowned upon, I turned to ChatGPT to quench my wanderlust. "Tell me about a weekend itinerary for Rome," I typed. It rolled out a detailed, virtual Roman holiday, complete with the Colosseum, the Vatican, and a cheesy pizza at Piazza Navona. As I roamed the streets of Rome from my living room, my only worry was about overstuffing myself with digital pasta.

Example prompt: "Tell me about a weekend itinerary for Rome within a budget of 600 Euros"

Use Case 4: The Weather Whiz

Don't get me wrong, I like surprises, but not when they pour down on my freshly ironed suit. On a hunch, I asked ChatGPT on Bing, "What's the weather like tomorrow?" The accurate forecast it provided allowed me to dodge the weather's watery bullets, saved me from a few embarrassing wet t-shirt contests.

Example prompt: "What's the weather like tomorrow?"

Use Case 5: The Financial Forecaster

I must confess, the world of stocks and investments gives me hives. One fine day, in a fit of ambition (or insanity), I decided to understand my investments. "Explain the difference between stocks, bonds and mutual funds" I asked ChatGPT. It proceeded to explain investment terms in simple English, leaving me with a clearer picture of my retirement fund (and minor heart palpitations at the ups and downs of the stock market).

Example prompt: "Explain the difference between stocks, bonds and mutual funds"

Use Case 6: The Meditative Mentor

Meditation always felt like an impossible feat, like trying to teach a cat to fetch. But I also wondered – are the benefits of meditation real or mostly imagined? One evening, I decided to explore this question. "ChatGPT, are the health benefits of meditation supported in the scientific literature?" I requested. ChatGPT quoted prominent scientific sources and studies in its answer (The answer is yes, they are real!).

Example prompt: "ChatGPT, are the health benefits of meditation supported in the scientific literature?"

Use Case 7: The Cybernetic Culinary Guide

Now, cooking isn't exactly my forte. I've been known to char toast and turn pasta into a gluey mess. So, I enlisted the help of ChatGPT, "Can you provide a simple recipe for chicken soup?" What I got was a step-by-step guide to a warm, hearty bowl of chicken soup that even I couldn't mess up. Let's just say, the kitchen fire department hasn't been called since.

Example prompt: "Can you provide a simple recipe for chicken soup?"

Use Case 8: The Fitness Fanatic

One morning, a reflection in the mirror shocked me - an uncanny resemblance to a well-fed panda. I decided to shake things up a bit. "ChatGPT, can you suggest a simple fitness routine?" I requested. It laid out a gentle yet effective fitness plan that didn't require me to turn my living room into a makeshift gym. My journey from panda to panther had begun.

Example prompt: "ChatGPT, can you suggest a simple fitness routine?"

As I sit back and reflect on my experiences, it's clear that my digital assistant, ChatGPT, is no ordinary AI. It's a cocktail of a secretary, travel agent, financial advisor, personal chef, and fitness guru, with a pinch of mindfulness coach thrown in for good measure. It's like having my personal Jeeves, always at my beck and call, without worrying about if it's shaken or stirred.

Chapter 10: The Machine Mediator- Making Peace, One Byte at a Time

Use Case 1: The Digital Diplomat

Once, in a moment of social calamity, I decided to conduct a family meeting over Thanksgiving dinner. Suffice it to say, the stuffing wasn't the only thing that got heated. The next day, nursing a bruised ego and an upset stomach, I turned to ChatGPT. "How can I resolve a family argument about politics?" The wise AI suggested finding common ground, listening more than speaking, and, above all, practicing empathy. To my surprise, my family responded positively, and we all agreed to keep politics off the menu at future holiday dinners.

Example prompt: "How can I resolve a family argument about politics?"

Use Case 2: The Virtual Confidant

Late one night, I found myself wrestling with a daunting dilemma. To dye my hair or not to dye my hair? What if I end up looking like a poodle that's just been electrocuted? I turned to ChatGPT for advice: "Should I color my hair at home?" ChatGPT provided a comprehensive pros and cons list, leaving me informed and relieved. It was like having a close friend at my fingertips - one who didn't sugarcoat things but was always supportive.

Example prompt: "Should I color my hair at home? Make a list of pros and cons."

Use Case 3: The Ghostwriter of Apologies

One can't deny the exquisite art of delivering an apology - a balancing act of words, where one misplaced syllable can result in disaster. During a moment of folly, I had hurt my neighbor's feelings. I turned to ChatGPT for help: "How can I apologize to my neighbor for my harsh words?" What it generated was a sincere, heartfelt apology that conveyed my remorse without sounding over-the-top or insincere. The result? My neighbor not only forgave me but also gifted me a basket of homemade muffins.

Example prompt: "How can I apologize to my neighbor for my harsh words?"

Use Case 4: The Peacekeeper at Work

When you're stuck between your boss and a hard place, you need more than a shot of whiskey. As my boss became increasingly unreasonable, I was on the brink of sending him a strongly worded email. Before hitting 'Send,' I asked ChatGPT: "How can I communicate my concerns to my boss without being confrontational?" The tactful response it suggested was nothing short of diplomatic brilliance. It allowed me to express my issues professionally while maintaining my dignity - and my job.

Example prompt: "How can I communicate my concerns to my boss without being confrontational?"

Use Case 5: The Cupid of the Digital Age

As an adventurous boomer, I once ventured into the strange world of online dating. When I matched with a potential suitor, I was stumped about how to start the conversation. "What should I write to my online match?" I asked ChatGPT.

The witty opener it suggested not only broke the ice but also initiated a riveting conversation. If only it could also prevent me from spilling spaghetti on my shirt during the first date.

Example prompt: "What are three examples of opening lines I could write to a new online dating match?"

Use Case 6: The Texting Tactician

In a world where a misplaced emoji can lead to a family feud, I felt like I was tiptoeing through a minefield. During one such perilous journey, I sought ChatGPT's assistance: "How can I decline a party invitation politely?" ChatGPT's response was a gracious yet firm refusal that would even impress Emily Post. Now, if only it could also make my pesky cousin understand that her '80s theme parties aren't my cup of tea.

Example prompt: "How can I decline a party invitation politely?"

Use Case 7: The Art of Gentle Rebuttals

While partaking in a spirited debate on the best James Bond actor (it's Sean Connery, no doubt), I found myself cornered by a zealous Roger Moore fan. Before I could blurt out something regrettable, I consulted ChatGPT: "How can I respectfully disagree with someone's opinion?" Its tactful response allowed me to stand my ground while maintaining respect. Thanks to ChatGPT, I'm a graceful debater - a pacifist armed with words.

Example prompt: "How can I respectfully disagree with someone's opinion?"

Use Case 8: Decoding Subtext

Have you ever received a text message that's as comprehensible as hieroglyphics? Welcome to my world. One evening, after receiving a cryptic text from my nephew, I turned to ChatGPT: "What does 'sorry for ghosting, I was swamped AF' mean?" The AI helped me decode the message without making me feel like a complete technophobe. Turns out, AF doesn't mean 'Always Friendly.' Who knew?

Example prompt: "What does 'sorry for ghosting, I was swamped AF' mean?"

In conclusion, with ChatGPT by my side, I've become quite the diplomat. I manage to keep my foot out of my mouth, and the taste of shoe leather is becoming an increasingly distant memory. From being a peacekeeper to a relationship navigator, ChatGPT is my go-to digital negotiator. It's like having a UN ambassador in my pocket, except it doesn't get jet-lagged or require fancy hors d'oeuvres.

Chapter 11: An AI for Your Health: The Unlikely Digital Doctor

Use Case 1: ChatGPT, the Med School Dropout

Let's start with an undeniable truth — ChatGPT didn't graduate from med school. Yet, it has a knack for medical tidbits that'll make a hypochondriac swoon. Feeling an odd twinge in your toe? "What could cause pain in my toe?" you ask ChatGPT. Next thing you know, you're reading about gout, fractures, and that trendy stiletto you've been squeezing your foot into.

But remember, ChatGPT isn't a doctor, so always consult with a healthcare professional if you're feeling unwell. As much as we wish it could, ChatGPT isn't about to perform a digital appendectomy.

Example prompt: "What could cause pain in my toe?"

Use Case 2: Demystifying Medical Mumbo Jumbo

There's a certain cruelty in the language of medicine. A minor bump on the head becomes a contusion, and before you know it, you're running for the hills. "What's a contusion?" you ask ChatGPT. And suddenly, a contusion doesn't seem quite so terrifying.

The AI doesn't gloat over your ignorance but treats you with patient understanding, transforming medical jargon into digestible English. Although it's no replacement for a heart-to-heart chat with your doctor, it does make those chats a little less daunting.

Example prompt: "What's a contusion?"

Use Case 3: The Low-Calorie Recipe Curator

Once upon a time, I decided to go on a diet. A decision as regrettable as my neon tube socks phase. But, armed with determination and a muffin top, I asked ChatGPT: "Give me a low-calorie dinner recipe." Its response was a mouthwatering roasted chicken with quinoa salad recipe that was a far cry from the rabbit food I had expected.

Since then, I've explored a cornucopia of low-calorie delights with my digital diet buddy. However, it's worth mentioning that ChatGPT is, sadly, unable to keep you from midnight refrigerator raids.

Example prompt: "Give me a low-calorie vegetarian dinner recipe."

Use Case 4: The Home Workout Guide

During a certain lockdown – which we won't talk about – I put on a little weight. Alright, a lot of weight. In a bout of self-consciousness, I turned to ChatGPT: "What's a good home workout routine for beginners?" The next moment, I was introduced to a regime of squats, planks, and something devilishly called a burpee.

ChatGPT, as it turned out, was a rather harsh digital personal trainer. Although it can't guilt you with judgmental stares like a real coach, it certainly keeps your muscles guessing.

Example prompt: "What's a good home workout routine for beginners?"

Use Case 5: The Yoga Pose Explainer

Embracing my inner zen master, I once decided to try yoga. But after a few unsuccessful attempts at the "downward facing dog," I looked more like an "upset cat." Desperate, I asked ChatGPT: "How can I properly do the downward-facing dog pose?" Its detailed description, complete with reminders about breathing, was nothing short of enlightening.

ChatGPT might not be a yogi, but it sure knows its Asanas from its Pranayamas. Just remember, it can't catch you if you fall out of that tree pose.

Example prompt: "How can I properly do the downward-facing dog yoga pose?"

Use Case 6: The Master of Mindful Meditation

During a stressful week, the kind where you'd prefer becoming a hermit crab, I sought solace in ChatGPT: "Can you guide me through a brief mindfulness meditation?" What followed was a soothing, step-by-step mindfulness exercise that felt like a spa treatment for the mind.

ChatGPT is an excellent mindfulness mentor, helping you navigate the tumultuous seas of stress with grace. But remember, it can't light your scented candles or prepare your herbal tea.

Example prompt: "Can you guide me through a brief mindfulness meditation – guiding me in the style of Ricky Gervais?"

Use Case 7: The Sleep Hygiene Guru

Sleep and I have a complicated relationship, like cats and vacuum cleaners. Out of desperation, I turned to ChatGPT: "How can I improve my sleep hygiene?" Its advice was a mix of sensible bedtimes, tech-free zones, and lavender-infused dreams.

Since then, my nights have been more restful, and my mornings less grumpy. ChatGPT might not be a dream weaver, but it certainly knows how to lull you towards sleep's sweet embrace.

Example prompt: "How can I improve my sleep hygiene?"

Use Case 8: The Fitness Progress Tracker

We're in a time where tracking fitness progress has become a crucial part of our exercise routine. It's easy to get lost amidst numerous exercises, personal bests, and set goals. So, one day, I asked ChatGPT: "How can I track my fitness progress effectively?" What it served up was a practical and comprehensive guide to record my performance, suggesting different methods like fitness apps, workout logs, and even mindful body observations.

In this fitness-focused era, ChatGPT emerges as a worthy companion. While it's not a personal trainer, its fitness advice is certainly more informed than that gym rat who insists on giving you unsolicited tips.

Example prompt: "How can I track my fitness progress effectively?"

In conclusion, though ChatGPT may not have a medical degree, its ability to offer valuable health-related information is commendable. Keep in mind, it's not a substitute for a real doctor, so please, don't ask it to diagnose your symptoms or interpret your lab results. Always consult a professional healthcare provider; they've spent years in med school and they know their business.

ChatGPT, my digital confidante, might lack a lab coat and a stethoscope, but it undeniably aids in navigating the intricate world of health and wellness, without making you feel embarrassed or overwhelmed. It's like having an informed friend at your beck and call, minus the obligatory coffee dates or the hassle of scheduling appointments.

Chapter 12: The Bot that Built a Bookshelf: ChatGPT in the Realm of DIY

Use Case 1: ChatGPT, the Tool Whisperer

My first brush with DIY didn't quite end well. In fact, it ended with me being on a first-name basis with the local ER staff. My half-built bookshelf stood in the corner, mocking me, while my thumb doubled in size and changed colors quicker than a chameleon in a bag of Skittles.

In a fit of frustration, I turned to ChatGPT: "How can I safely use a hammer without smashing my thumb?" Its reply was precise, detailing the correct grip, positioning, and technique to prevent further hammer mishaps. Now, if only I had asked that question a thumb-ache earlier.

Example prompt: "How can I safely use a hammer without smashing my thumb?"

Use Case 2: The Hardware Connoisseur

In the past, whenever I walked into a hardware store, I felt like I had wandered into an alien landscape. Rows upon rows of nuts, bolts, screws, and tools, each with their own cryptic names and purpose. I'd usually walk out with a handful of items, hoping that I had what I needed for my next DIY project.

One day, I decided to seek ChatGPT's help: "What tools and materials do I need to build a bookshelf?" ChatGPT's response was a detailed list of tools and materials, from the type and size of wood needed, to the specific screws and the tools I'd need to put it all together.

Since then, my trips to the hardware store have been less daunting. ChatGPT might not be able to wield a hammer or saw, but it definitely knows its way around a toolshed.

Example prompt: "What tools and materials do I need to build a bookshelf?"

Use Case 3: The Paint Color Consultant

Picking a paint color is like choosing a favorite child. You're torn, guilty, and everyone's judging your decision. When I decided to repaint my living room, the color options made my head spin like a top.

Turning to my AI friend, I queried, "ChatGPT, what color should I paint my living room?" Considering the room's size, natural lighting, and my personal taste, it recommended a soothing sage green. And I must say, the choice was spot-on. If you ever visit, bring your sunglasses; the tastefulness is blinding.

Example prompt: "ChatGPT, what color should I paint my living room? What factors should I tell you about to make a great suggestion?"

Use Case 4: The Plumbing Guide

Plumbing and I have a love-hate relationship. I hate it, and it loves to make me miserable. When my sink decided to impersonate Old Faithful, I had a minor breakdown.

Desperate, I asked ChatGPT, "How can I fix a leaking sink?" Its reply was a step-by-step guide that made me feel like a knight facing a dragon… a very wet dragon. Twenty minutes later, I emerged victorious, only slightly damp, and my sink returned to its non-volcanic behavior.

Example prompt: "How can I fix a leaking sink?"

Use Case 5: The IKEA Furniture Assembler

My first IKEA furniture assembly experience was a saga of epic proportions. I was left with a half-assembled bed, a pile of mysterious screws, and a severely wounded pride.

Feeling beaten, I turned to ChatGPT: "What websites can I use to find someone to assemble my IKEA furniture?" I was provided with a list of websites where I could find freelancers, with a list of pros and cons for each website.

Example prompt: "What websites can I use to find someone to assemble my IKEA furniture?"

Use Case 6: The Upcycling Advocate

One man's trash is another man's treasure, they say. But all I saw in my dusty attic was an empire of junk. Until I asked ChatGPT, "What can I do with these old wooden crates?" Its suggestions for upcycling projects were an eye-opener, transforming my crates into chic rustic shelves and charming planters.

Now, my friends ogle my upcycled wonders, while I bask in my newfound eco-conscious creativity. My attic, however, is still an empire of junk. One victory at a time, I suppose.

Example prompt: "What can I do with three large old wooden crates?"

Use Case 7: The Green Energy Advisor

In my pursuit to embrace greener living, I decided to install solar panels. The technical jargon, though, made it seem like I was reading an alien user manual.

Asking ChatGPT, "What do the terms 'Photovoltaic', 'Inverter' and 'Polycrystalline' mean in relation to solar panels – please explain as if you're talking to a child." it demystified the jargon for me. I now have solar panels on my roof and a planet-friendly smugness in my stride.

Example prompt: "What do the terms 'Photovoltaic', 'Inverter' and 'Polycrystalline' mean in relation to solar panels – please explain as if you're talking to a child."

Use Case 8: The Home Safety Auditor

From fire safety to burglary prevention, securing a home is a full-time job. I asked ChatGPT, "What are the best ways to secure my home?" Its comprehensive list of safety measures, from smoke detectors to motion-sensing lights, turned my humble abode into a fortress.

With ChatGPT as my guide in the wild world of DIY, I've hammered, painted, plumbed, assembled, upcycled, installed, and secured my way through countless projects. But remember, ChatGPT can't physically help you carry that heavy bookshelf or rescue you from a plumbing mishap. For those tasks, enlist the help of a willing (or easily bribed) friend.

Example prompt: "What are the best ways to secure my home?"

Its knowledge is impressive, its patience endless, but please, don't ask it to hold the ladder for you or pass you the wrench. We're still a few technological leaps away from a ChatGPT butler-bot. So, until then, it's just you, your two hands, and an AI that somehow makes you believe you can build Rome in a day.

Chapter 13: The Literary Leaps and Loops of ChatGPT: A Digital Book Club

Use Case 1: The Reading Recipient

The name is David. And I am a book snob. It's true. If a book doesn't pique my interest in the first three sentences, it's tossed aside faster than a New Year's resolution. So naturally, I turned to my digital confidante, ChatGPT, and demanded, "Recommend a book that will knock my socks off." It conjured up a list of masterpieces, each with a brief, tantalizing synopsis. I grudgingly admit that my socks were, indeed, blown off.

Example prompt: "Recommend a crime fiction book that will knock my socks off."

Use Case 2: The Tricky Translation Tutor

I adore French literature, but my French comprehension is on par with my understanding of quantum physics. It's all Greek to me, but French. I once asked ChatGPT, "Can you translate this line from 'Les Misérables' for me?" The result? My very own bilingual co-conspirator in my literary crimes. Now, Victor Hugo and I share whispers in the night, thanks to my trusty AI translator.

Example prompt: "Can you translate this line from 'Les Misérables' for me?"

Use Case 3: The Contextual Clue Detective

Reading an old English novel is like navigating a labyrinth in a fog, blindfolded, with a slightly tipsy Minotaur. The jargon! The social context! The absurdly large bonnets! In sheer

desperation, I asked ChatGPT, "What on earth does this line from 'Pride and Prejudice' mean?" Its clarification was like a lighthouse in the foggy sea of bonnets and genteel sarcasm.
Example prompt: "What on earth does this line from 'Pride and Prejudice' mean?"

Use Case 4: The Poetic Perception Provider
Ah, poetry! The pure, distilled essence of human emotion! Or so they say. To me, it's more like a jigsaw puzzle with half the pieces missing and the other half on fire. One day, I handed a particularly confounding poem to ChatGPT, "What is this poet trying to say?" What followed was a patient explanation that pieced together the puzzle, extinguished the fire, and even made the poem feel... profound.
Example prompt: "What is this poet trying to say?"

Use Case 5: The Literary Critic
It's not enough to read a book; we must dissect it, analyze it, and then reassemble it. A veritable Frankenstein's monster of literary critique. During one such session, I turned to ChatGPT, "What are the themes in 'To Kill a Mockingbird'?" Its response was an enlightening discussion that made me see the novel in a new light, while also making me feel slightly smarter.
Example prompt: "What are the themes in 'To Kill a Mockingbird'?"

Use Case 6: The Fan-Fiction Facilitator
Let's admit it. We all have wished for different endings to our favorite stories, or at least dreamt up some scintillating plot twists. On one such occasion, I asked ChatGPT, "What if

Romeo and Juliet lived?" What it spun was a fan-fiction that was Shakespearean yet unique, tragic yet hopeful. It was like peering into an alternate universe where, contrary to all historical evidence, star-crossed lovers don't have to meet tragic ends.

Example prompt: "What if Romeo and Juliet lived?"

Use Case 7: The Incessant Idea Incubator

Every writer, at some point, faces the dread of a blank page. The white, empty expanse of nothingness. During my showdown with the blank page, I asked ChatGPT, "What should I write about?" Its suggestions were a delightful buffet of story prompts, character ideas, and plot twists. With a sigh of relief, I bid adieu to the blank page and hello to a brewing storm of a story.

Example prompt: "What should I write about?"

Use Case 8: The Authorial Advisor

I fancy myself a writer, and my first draft was as promising as a cat playing the piano. Terribly amusing, but far from Mozart. In my despair, I asked ChatGPT, "How can I improve my writing?" Its constructive critique, encouraging words, and practical suggestions were akin to a personal writing coach, minus the exorbitant fees and awkward coffee meetings.

Example prompt: "Here is an example of my writing, please provide tips to improve my writing."

In the hallowed halls of the ChatGPT book club, I've discovered, explored, dissected, and even created literature. The smell of old paper and ink might be missing, but it's replaced by the stimulating scent of digital knowledge and unlimited possibilities. I can't help but picture ChatGPT in a cozy cardigan, glasses perched on its non-existent nose, engrossed in a digital tome, ready to turn the page and dive into the next literary adventure with me.

Chapter 14: Melodies, Beats, and AI: The Unexpected Music Maestro

Use Case 1: The Playlist Prognosticator

Back in my day, the height of technological music prowess was a Walkman. Yes, the cassette-playing, belt-holstering Walkman. And making a mixtape? It was an art, a delicate balance between music, static, and the ever-looming risk of the cassette tape unspooling into a tangled mess. The youth today, they wouldn't know that agony.

One day, tired of the Spotify algorithm recommending me the same three songs (Yes, I get it, I like "Hotel California"), I turned to my digital bard, ChatGPT. "Recommend me some new songs," I demanded. And lo and behold, it created a list. Not just any list, but a thoughtfully crafted sequence of songs spanning genres, decades, and continents. It was like a mixtape made by a friend who knows you better than you know yourself. And the best part? No fear of tangled cassette tapes.

Example prompt: "Recommend me some new songs. My favourite song is 'Hotel California'."

Use Case 2: The Sonic Soothsayer

Once, I found myself in a particular funk. One of those moods where everything feels as gray as a pigeon in a cityscape. In desperation, I asked ChatGPT, "What music will cheer me up?" What followed was an upbeat, uplifting playlist that had me tapping my feet and dancing in my living room like an extra in a 'Footloose' remake. I've since decided that ChatGPT is my personal DJ, armed with the uncanny ability to match melodies to moods.

Example prompt: "What music will cheer me up?"

Use Case 3: The Lyric Librarian

Remember when you'd have a song stuck in your head, just one line of it, and it would gnaw at you until you finally remembered the title or artist? One such earworm had lodged itself in my brain, driving me up the wall and down the other side. I scribbled out some of the lyrics I remembered to ChatGPT, "Do you know this song?" In response, it presented not only the song title and artist but also the complete lyrics. It's like having a walking, talking (typing?) encyclopedia of every song lyric known to humankind.

Example prompt: "Do you know this song? I remember these lyrics…"

Use Case 4: The Music History Hermit

Ever found yourself wanting to impress a group of friends or, better yet, a date, with your extensive knowledge of music history? Just me? Well, regardless, ChatGPT is the perfect companion for such ambitions. When I once asked, "Tell me more about the history of jazz," what I received was a thorough, engaging history of the genre, complete with the key figures, landmark events, and even the societal context of the era. You may not be able to teach an old dog new tricks, but you can teach it some pretty impressive trivia.

Example prompt: "Tell me more about the history of jazz"

Use Case 5: The Songbird Simulator

Music isn't just about listening; it's about creating. Now, I'm no Mozart, and my singing voice is what people diplomatically call "distinctive." But one night, feeling particularly ambitious, I asked ChatGPT, "Help me write a song." What followed was a collaborative session that resulted in a song. My song. Our song. While it may not top the charts, it was distinctly mine, and the joy of creation was pure magic.

Example prompt: "Help me write a pop song about birds and love."

Use Case 6: The Instrument Instructor

My relationship with musical instruments is best described as 'it's complicated.' I have a guitar gathering dust in the corner, a reminder of my failed attempts at mastering it. So, it was with a heavy heart that I asked ChatGPT, "How do I play a C chord?" Its patient explanation was like a gentle guitar teacher who, unlike human teachers, doesn't wince when you hit the wrong note.

Example prompt: "How do I play a C chord?"

Use Case 7: The Band Biographer

Curiosity about a band or artist doesn't stop at their music; it extends to their history, their origins, and their journey. Upon asking ChatGPT, "Tell me about The Beatles," I found myself reading a concise but engaging narrative of the Fab Four, their rise to fame, their discography, and their impact on popular culture. It was like a VH1 documentary but without the exaggerated dramatic reenactments.

Example prompt: "Tell me about The Beatles"

Use Case 8: The Concert Connoisseur

As a self-proclaimed concert junkie, there's nothing quite like the thrill of live music. Sadly, my days of mosh pits are behind me, but that doesn't mean I can't enjoy a good gig. When asked ChatGPT via Bing, "Find upcoming concerts in my area," ChatGPT obliges with a list of shows, complete with dates, venues, and ticket links. It's like having a music-savvy buddy who always knows what's going on in town.

Example prompt: "Find upcoming concerts in my area"

In conclusion, ChatGPT is a Maestro, Librarian, Historian, Instructor, Biographer, and Connoisseur. It's a symphony of knowledge and assistance, ready to step into any role in your musical journey. But don't just take my word for it. Ask it to suggest a song, write a tune, explain a chord, or find a gig. Who knows, you might just discover a whole new rhythm to your life, one AI-generated beat at a time.

Chapter 15: The Machine's Guide to the Internet: Exploring the Digital Jungle with an AI Sidekick

Use Case 1: The Search Engine Whisperer

It started with a simple query, "Who won the Oscar for Best Actor in 1995?" A straightforward question for a human, an even more straightforward one for ChatGPT. Like a loyal hunting dog, it promptly fetched the answer - Tom Hanks, for 'Forrest Gump,' if you're curious. It was my first glimpse of ChatGPT as an internet sleuth, a digital detective that cuts through the chaos of the World Wide Web.

Example prompt: "Who won the Oscar for Best Actor in 1995?"

Use Case 2: The Keeper of the Meme Lore

The internet, as I understand, runs on memes - digital tidbits that spread like wildfire and are as fickle as a cat on a hot tin roof. Just when I'm getting the hang of "Doge" and "Pepe the Frog," the internet has moved on to the next sensation. In a bid to keep up, I asked ChatGPT, "Explain the latest memes to me?" And boy, did it deliver! It not only explained the newest meme trend but also provided the cultural context that made it funny. Who knew AI had a sense of humor?

Example prompt: "Explain the latest memes to me including Doge and Pepe the Frog – why do the young generation like them?"

Use Case 3: The Urban Dictionary Savant

Internet slang is another area where I perpetually feel out of depth. It's like everyone's speaking in a secret code, and I've misplaced my decoder ring. Feeling a bit sheepish, I turned to ChatGPT, "What does 'on fleek' mean?" It patiently explained the term without an ounce of judgment. It's like having a cool, younger cousin who helps you navigate the modern lexicon without making fun of your lack of knowledge.

Example prompt: "What does 'on fleek' mean?"

Use Case 4: The Social Media Sentinel

In the confusing world of hashtags, trending topics, and viral posts, I felt lost, like a kid who wandered away from his parents at the state fair. Desperate to understand the latest Twitter storm, I asked ChatGPT on Bing, "What is trending on Twitter, and why?" It translated the whirlwind of tweets into coherent, comprehensible language. It was like having my personal interpreter for the bewildering Babel that is social media.

Example prompt: "What is trending on Twitter, and why?"

Use Case 5: The WebMD that Doesn't Induce Panic

We've all been there, turning to the internet in a fevered panic after noticing a strange rash or a persistent cough. Usually, the internet's verdict ranges from a common cold to some exotic, terminal illness. Tired of self-diagnosing myself into a frenzy, I asked ChatGPT, "What are the symptoms of common cold?" It offered a balanced, well-researched answer that soothed my nerves. It felt like talking to a kind, patient nurse instead of diving headfirst into the anxiety-ridden abyss of online health forums.

Example prompt: "What are the symptoms of common cold?"

Use Case 6: The AI for DIY

YouTube is a goldmine of DIY videos. But when you're looking to fix a leaky faucet, the last thing you want is to wade through hours of footage where someone tells their life story before getting to the actual faucet-fixing part. Out of desperation, I asked ChatGPT, "How do I fix a leaky faucet?" It responded with a step-by-step, no-nonsense guide, which made me feel like the Bob the Builder of the Boomer generation.

Example prompt: "How do I fix a leaky faucet?"

Use Case 7: The Eloquent Email Assistant

Writing an email might seem like a simple task, but when you're trying to word a complaint or request without sounding like a jerk, it becomes a Herculean task. Frustrated, I turned to ChatGPT, "Help me write a complaint email to my internet provider." It came back with a polite, firm, and articulate email draft that would have made Emily Post proud. It's like having an etiquette expert and a secretary all rolled into one.

Example prompt: "Help me write a complaint email to my internet provider."

Use Case 8: The AI Movie Buff

In the streaming age, picking a movie or a TV series is more daunting than browsing the aisles of Blockbuster on a Friday night. Overwhelmed by choice, I asked ChatGPT, "Suggest a good mystery movie." It suggested a few options based on popular ratings and reviews, saving me from the endless scrolling and previewing. It felt like having a movie-savvy friend who knows just the right film for your mood.

Example prompt: "Suggest a good mystery movie."

In conclusion, ChatGPT is your sherpa for the digital Everest that is the internet. It decodes the cryptic lingo, it curates your movie night, it guides you through DIY projects, and it keeps you updated on the latest trends, memes, and Twitter storms. It's your pocket guide to the digital jungle, ready to leap into action at a moment's notice. Just ask it to explain a meme, suggest a movie, or draft an email. Who knows, you might just find yourself feeling less like an internet newbie and more like a digital native. And all it takes is a simple chat with an AI.

Chapter 16: Your Virtual Shopping Assistant: Diving into the Digital Marketplace with ChatGPT

Use Case 1: The Cyberspace Bargain Hunter

Online shopping - it's like walking into a store with a blindfold on. Sure, there are pictures and descriptions, but who really knows what you're getting until it shows up on your doorstep, right? Well, it seems I found a trusty sidekick to guide me through the labyrinth of eCommerce. When I asked ChatGPT on Bing, "Where can I find the best deal for a KitchenAid mixer?" it spat out a list of sites with current prices and deals. It was like having my own personal bargain hunter, sans the awful fluorescent lighting of a clearance sale.

Example prompt: "Where can I find the best deal for a KitchenAid mixer?"

Use Case 2: The Outfit Orchestrator

Fashion was never my strong suit. Back in my day, a good outfit was a clean shirt and pants that didn't embarrass your mother. But now, with all these terms like "athleisure" and "normcore," I feel like I've walked into a foreign film without subtitles. So, I asked ChatGPT, "What's a fashionable outfit for a 60-year-old man?" In no time, it crafted a list of items that made me sound like the next GQ model. No cap, that's what the kids say, right?

Example prompt: "What's a fashionable outfit for a 60-year-old man?"

Use Case 3: The Sneakerhead Sidekick

I was tasked with getting my grandson a pair of "cool sneakers" for his birthday. Now, unless "cool" means "comfortable and sensibly priced," I was out of my depth. Panicked, I turned to ChatGPT, "What's a popular sneaker for teenagers?" ChatGPT listed a few trendy models, explained why they were popular, and even suggested a few places where I could find them. Suddenly, I was the hip grandparent with an uncanny knack for gifting.

Example prompt: "What's a popular sneaker for teenagers?"

Use Case 4: The Sentimental Gifter

My wife and I were celebrating our golden anniversary, and I wanted to gift her something unique and heartfelt. As much as I wanted to avoid the cliché of jewelry, I wasn't sure what would capture the magnitude of our journey together. Desperate, I asked ChatGPT, "What's a meaningful anniversary gift for my wife?" ChatGPT suggested a custom star map of the night we first met. I must admit, even I was impressed by the romantic genius of this AI.

Example prompt: "What's a meaningful anniversary gift for my wife?"

Use Case 5: The Critic of Fine Wines and Cheeses

When you're asked to bring wine to a dinner party, it's like being handed a live grenade. One wrong move, and you're the bozo who brought the terrible wine. So, to avoid that, I asked ChatGPT, "What's a good wine to pair with brie cheese?" It suggested a crisp Chardonnay and explained the nuances of the pairing. I entered the party, wine in hand, feeling like the suave host of a gourmet cooking show.

Example prompt: "What's a good wine to pair with brie cheese?"

Use Case 6: The Gadget Guru

Purchasing electronics these days feels like deciphering an alien language. I needed a new laptop, but all the talk about RAM, SSD, and GPU had me spinning. Confused, I asked ChatGPT, "What laptop should I buy for basic web browsing and word processing?" It recommended a few models, explained the features in plain English, and even suggested where I could get the best deal. It's like having a tech-savvy nephew who doesn't roll his eyes at your questions.

Example prompt: "What sorts of laptops should I consider buy for basic web browsing and word processing?"

Use Case 7: The Savvy Plant Shopper

After a few failed attempts at indoor gardening (may those poor ferns rest in peace), I wanted to try my hand at something more...unkillable. I asked ChatGPT, "What's a hard-to-kill houseplant, and where can I buy it?" ChatGPT suggested the Snake Plant, listed its care instructions, and pointed me to a few online plant shops. Suddenly, I was not just a potential plant parent, but a potential plant parent who could keep his plants alive!

Example prompt: "What's a hard-to-kill houseplant, and where can I buy it?"

Use Case 8: The Magic 8-Ball of Subscriptions

Subscription boxes – another one of those modern wonders. It's like Christmas morning every month, but instead of Uncle Bob's dubious homemade pickles, you get things you might actually like. When I asked ChatGPT, "What's a good subscription box for a movie buff?" it suggested a few options, each with a brief description and why it would suit a cinephile. Now, every month feels like a mini film festival in my living room.

Example prompt: "What's a good subscription box for a movie buff?"

In conclusion, ChatGPT is your savvy companion in the vast and sometimes intimidating realm of online shopping. It hunts down deals, guides you through the latest trends, and even sparks your creativity for heartfelt gifts. With its help, you can navigate the digital marketplace like a pro, armed with information and confident in your choices. So, go ahead, ask it to suggest a gift, recommend a wine, or decode the enigma of electronics specs. With ChatGPT at your side, online shopping becomes less of a gamble and more of an adventure.

Chapter 17: ChatGPT, the Trivia Partner: A Night at the Quiz with a Computer Savant

Use Case 1: The Unexpected Rain Man

Did you ever watch that film "Rain Man?" You know, Dustin Hoffman counts toothpicks in a flash and bam, instant hit at the Blackjack table? Well, I always figured that if I had a human calculator by my side, pub quizzes wouldn't be the frustrating exercise in humility they usually are.

I asked ChatGPT, "Who won the 1969 World Series?" It didn't bat a pixelated eye before replying, "The New York Mets." If only I could drag it to my weekly trivia nights, my buddies would be convinced I had somehow become a walking encyclopedia overnight.

Example prompt: "Who won the 1969 World Series?"

Use Case 2: The Pop Culture Maestro

My granddaughter is into some strange-sounding bands these days. She tried to test my pop culture knowledge, asking me if I knew the lead singer of the Arctic Monkeys. To her surprise, I replied with "Alex Turner," all thanks to my trusty ChatGPT. I even threw in a fun fact about their debut album that I picked up from my AI friend. For once, I wasn't just the grandfather trying to keep up with the times; I was the cool grandpa who knew a thing or two about the hip kids on the block.

Example prompt: "Who is the lead singer of the Arctic Monkeys?"

Use Case 3: The Geography Whizz

Every year during our family reunions, we have a tradition - a global trivia challenge. This year, our smarty pants cousin from Yale tossed a doozy, "What's the capital of Burkina Faso?" Instead of looking like a deer in the headlights, I coolly replied, "Ouagadougou," courtesy of ChatGPT. To be honest, I didn't even know there was a country named Burkina Faso until that point.

Example prompt: "What's the capital of Burkina Faso?"

Use Case 4: The Science Nerd

My son-in-law is an astrophysicist, and at dinner parties, he enjoys throwing around questions about black holes and quantum mechanics to make us all feel a bit dim. I asked ChatGPT, "What is a quark?" I was given a fairly simple explanation about these elementary particles. At the next dinner, I casually used the term in conversation, much to the surprise of my son-in-law. He almost choked on his Brussels sprouts.

Example prompt: "What is a quark?"

Use Case 5: The Movie Buff

The folks at the local senior center decided to start a film trivia night, which, let me tell you, is about as chaotic as a room full of kittens and laser pointers. "Who won the Best Actress Oscar in 1973?" someone hollered from the back. In what's becoming a common theme, I played the hero, responding with "Glenda Jackson for 'A Touch of Class'," a fact I'd picked up from ChatGPT.

Example prompt: "Who won the Best Actress Oscar in 1973?"

Use Case 6: The Sports Statistician

Once, I was watching a baseball game with my friend Jim, a guy who knows stats like nobody's business. He asked me, "Who holds the record for the most home runs in a single season?" I was about to change the topic when I remembered I could ask ChatGPT. It informed me that Barry Bonds holds the record with 73 home runs in 2001. The look on Jim's face? Priceless.

Example prompt: "Who holds the record for the most home runs in a single season?"

Use Case 7: The History Buff

My niece had a history project on Ancient Egypt. She was stuck on a question about the construction of the pyramids. I asked ChatGPT, "How were the pyramids of Egypt built?" ChatGPT presented a detailed explanation about the possible construction methods and theories, which we used to finish her project. I must say, that AI has a knack for making history sound more interesting than any of my old school textbooks.

Example prompt: "How were the pyramids of Egypt built?"

Use Case 8: The Literary Know-It-All

During our monthly book club meeting, we had a heated debate about the author of "Pride and Prejudice." Most members were sure it was Charles Dickens. I politely disagreed, claiming it was Jane Austen - thanks, of course, to a quick check with ChatGPT. Suddenly, I was the literature guru. I'm still riding high on that wave of admiration.

Example prompt: "Who was the author of Pride and Prejudice?"

In conclusion, trivia night with ChatGPT is a hoot. Whether it's sports stats, history facts, or the latest pop culture trends, this AI can make you the star of any quiz night. It's the ultimate sidekick for anyone who's ever dreamed of knowing a little bit about everything. Trust me, it's fun to go from "the old man who gets every question wrong" to "the elder statesman of trivia." All you need is ChatGPT, and maybe a nice hat. Everyone respects a nice hat.

Chapter 18: The Home Organization Aid: An Odyssey into the Chaos and Order with ChatGPT

Use Case 1: The Titanic Toy Room Tangle

When my grandson invited me into his room, I wasn't expecting to embark on an adventure akin to discovering the lost city of Atlantis. "Welcome to my world, grandpa," he said, and I felt like Howard Carter entering Tutankhamun's tomb, except the treasures here were Lego blocks, action figures, and a hazardous assortment of tiny cars.

Desperate, I asked ChatGPT for help, "How can I organize a child's room?" It responded with a thorough strategy, including suggestions on using storage bins, categorizing toys, and involving the child in the process. It even recommended turning the cleanup into a game. Well, after three adventurous hours and a mock pirate treasure hunt, we emerged victorious. Order was restored, and I didn't even step on a Lego!

Example prompt: "How can I organize a child's room?"

Use Case 2: The Great Garage Groan

My wife, bless her heart, has a unique relationship with the garage. To her, it's a magical space where unwanted items vanish. To me, it's the beast's lair from the fairy tale 'Beauty and the Beast' — intimidating, monstrous, and filled with cursed antiques.

Asking ChatGPT, "What's the best way to declutter a garage?" was a step taken in desperation. The AI proceeded to outline a detailed plan, complete with sorting, categorizing, repurposing, and the holy grail of all advice: "don't buy more stuff than you can store." The transformation of our garage from a dumping ground to a neat storage area was a sight to behold. I even found my long-lost golf clubs!

Example prompt: "What's the best way to declutter a garage?"

Use Case 3: The Attic Adventure

A trip to the attic is like a journey back in time. Old photographs, stacks of books, dust-coated furniture... and don't get me started on the Christmas decorations! It's the embodiment of nostalgia and chaos combined. It's like diving headfirst into a temporal whirlpool filled with ornaments and mothballs.

With trepidation, I asked ChatGPT, "How can I sort and clean an attic?" The advice I received could put Marie Kondo to shame. It explained how to sort items by their sentimental and practical value, how to properly store old photos and documents, and ways to effectively use the attic space. After a day of work, my attic had morphed from a time-traveling junkyard to a well-arranged museum of family memorabilia.

Example prompt: "How can I sort and clean an attic?"

Use Case 4: The Cupboard Conundrum

Kitchen cupboards are the Las Vegas of the home. What happens in the cupboards, stays in the cupboards. Hidden behind those wooden doors, the food containers party, the spices run wild, and the canned goods form rebellious gangs.

I asked ChatGPT, "Any tips on organizing a kitchen cupboard?" The AI provided a comprehensive plan, from utilizing lazy susans and spice racks to tips on grouping items based on their usage and size. After following its advice, opening my cupboard is no longer a gamble. Now, the food containers sit in serene harmony, the spices huddle in neat rows, and the canned goods stand at attention like dutiful soldiers.

Example prompt: "Any tips on organizing a kitchen cupboard?"

Use Case 5: The Wardrobe War

If wardrobes could talk, mine would probably ask for a vacation. I mean, it's hard enough to maintain order when it's just shirts and trousers, but when you add ties, belts, and socks to the mix, chaos reigns.

Out of desperation, I asked ChatGPT, "How to organize my wardrobe?" Its response could've been taken straight out of a professional organizer's playbook. From folding techniques and the use of drawer separators, to organizing clothes by season or color, it left no stone unturned. By the end of the day, my wardrobe was a testament to order and efficiency.

Example prompt: "How can I organize my wardrobe according to the principles of Hygge?"

Use Case 6: The Basement Blues

I've always found basements to be wonderfully mysterious. They're like the house's subconscious, holding all the stuff we want to forget. Mine had become a wilderness, home to old tools, discarded appliances, and remnants of past hobbies.

So, I asked ChatGPT, "What's a good way to clean and organize a basement?" The plan it provided included useful tips like allocating different zones for different types of items and how to safely store old tools and appliances. After a few days of sweat and dust, my basement became more than a forgotten storage space, it turned into a useable, well-organized area.

Example prompt: "What's a good way to clean and organize a basement according to the principles of ikigai?"

Use Case 7: The Digital Disaster

Home organization isn't all about physical stuff. My computer files were another mess I had to tackle. From cryptically named documents to the labyrinthine folder structures, my desktop was a digital jungle.

So, I asked ChatGPT, "How can I declutter my digital space?" Its answer ranged from deleting unnecessary files, organizing files into folders, and making use of cloud storage to backing up important files and keeping the desktop clean. Now, my digital world is as tidy as my physical one, and I don't need a machete to navigate through my files.

Example prompt: "How can I declutter my digital space?"

Use Case 8: The Living Room Logic

My living room has seen more configurations than a Rubik's cube. Furniture moved, ornaments shifted, even the TV has had a few adventures of its own. But I never seemed to get it quite right.

In a final plea, I asked ChatGPT, "What's a good way to arrange my living room?" The AI suggested thinking about the room's primary function, considering the natural flow of traffic, balancing the furniture, and being mindful of lighting. Today, my living room finally makes sense, providing both comfort and style.

Example prompt: "What's are some good ways to arrange my living room?"

To sum up, I can say that ChatGPT, my ever-helpful AI assistant, has been the guiding light in my odyssey from chaos to order. From the toy-ridden room of my grandson to the wild realm of my garage, the nostalgically cluttered attic to the disorderly cupboards, the overstuffed wardrobe to the mysterious basement, and from my digital jungle to the Rubik's cube of my living room, ChatGPT has proven to be the compass, the map, and the wisdom I needed to navigate it all. Now, if only it could help me find my glasses…

Chapter 19: ChatGPT, the Event Planner: From Tea Parties to Titanic Shindigs

Use Case 1: The Great Granddaughter's Tea Party Extravaganza

I confess, the idea of throwing a tea party for my six-year-old great-granddaughter was as frightening as being chased by a rabid squirrel. What do I know about princesses, unicorns, and the correct way to serve imaginary tea? In sheer panic, I asked ChatGPT, "How to organize a tea party for kids?" The AI listed out everything from the party theme, decorations, snacks, and activities to maintaining a polite conversation with an invisible unicorn. It even suggested a princess etiquette lesson to make the kids feel royal. My great-granddaughter declared it "the best tea party ever!" and, believe me, that's a high honor coming from a discerning princess.

Example prompt: "How to organize a tea party for kids?"

Use Case 2: The Wife's Surprise Birthday Bash

The phrase "surprise party" is as nerve-wracking as "IRS audit". But it was my wife's milestone birthday, and I wanted to do something special. So I asked ChatGPT, "How to plan a surprise birthday party?" The AI gave an organized breakdown of the process, including guest list creation, venue selection, menu planning, and diversion tactics. It even provided ideas on party themes and decoration tips. When my wife walked into her 1950s-themed surprise party, the look on her face was worth every stressful moment.

Example prompt: "How to plan a surprise birthday party?"

Use Case 3: The Neighborhood Block Party Saga

Someone once told me, "The best way to meet your neighbors is to throw a block party." So I asked ChatGPT, "How to organize a neighborhood block party?" Its suggestions ranged from securing a permit, setting a date and time, organizing games, to planning a potluck menu. Following its advice, I even set up a neighborhood band, starring yours truly on the harmonica. The block party was a hit, and we all discovered that the grumpy man at the end of the street has a killer karaoke voice!

Example prompt: "How to organize a neighborhood block party?"

Use Case 4: The Housewarming Hullabaloo

Moving to a new home is a big event, and it deserves a celebration. I asked ChatGPT, "How to plan a housewarming party?" It provided tips for sending invites, setting up a tour of the new home, arranging snacks and drinks, and even suggestions for a fun playlist. The party was a success, and my guests left with full stomachs and a comprehensive knowledge of my home's square footage and the benefits of open-plan living.

Example prompt: "How to plan a housewarming party?"

Use Case 5: The Yard Sale Caper

In an attempt to downsize, I decided to host a yard sale. I asked ChatGPT, "How to organize a successful yard sale?" It gave step-by-step instructions on everything from sorting items, pricing them appropriately, advertising the sale, to setting up the display. The yard sale was more popular than a summer ice-cream truck, and I managed to rehome everything from my beloved lawnmower to that monstrous ceramic vase Aunt Edna gifted us for our wedding.

Example prompt: "How to organize a successful yard sale?"

Use Case 6: The Disaster-Proof Barbecue

Summers are for barbecues, but my grill skills are about as refined as a bull in a china shop. Hoping to avoid any emergency services this time, I asked ChatGPT, "How to plan a summer barbecue?" The AI provided a checklist, ranging from the choice of meats, to recipes for marinades, to setting up a comfortable seating arrangement. It even had tips on grill safety. The barbecue was a culinary triumph, and my eyebrows remained intact!

Example prompt: "How to plan a summer barbecue?"

Use Case 7: The Family Reunion Rumble

Organizing a family reunion is like directing a multigenerational, chaotic theater play. So I asked ChatGPT, "How to plan a family reunion?" The AI delivered a comprehensive guide including suggestions on selecting a date and venue, creating an itinerary, arranging catering, and planning activities suitable for all ages. The reunion was such a hit that even Uncle Lou, who generally can't bear social events, was the last to leave!

Example prompt: "How to plan a family reunion?"

Use Case 8: The Retirement Party Production

When a colleague announced their retirement, I was assigned the task of planning the party. I asked ChatGPT, "How to organize a retirement party?" The AI suggested everything from deciding on a suitable theme, creating a memorable program, inviting the retiree's family, and collecting stories and messages from colleagues. There wasn't a dry eye in the house when we presented the retiree with a memory book full of messages from their coworkers.
Example prompt: "How to organize a retirement party?"

In summary, be it a tea party for my discerning great-granddaughter or a blockbuster neighborhood block party, a surprise birthday bash or a housewarming hullabaloo, a yard sale or a barbecue, a family reunion or a heart-touching retirement party, ChatGPT had my back. With its trusty advice and handy checklists, I felt like I was wearing a super-planner cape. Who knew I'd transform from an event-planning novice to a veritable party maestro with the help of a few gigabytes of code? With this newfound power, who knows, I might just start planning Christmas in June!

Chapter 20: ChatGPT, the Professional Consultant: Suit Up and Level Up

Use Case 1: The Unlikely Job Seeker

As my granddaughter prepared to venture into the job market, fresh out of college, I wanted to play the sagacious grandparent role, so I asked ChatGPT, "What advice should I give to a new graduate seeking employment?" ChatGPT volleyed back with a list of insights that made me feel like a fortune cookie guru: "Networking is key," "Customize your resume for each job," "Practice your interview skills," and "Consider internships." At our next Sunday dinner, I dropped these wisdom bombs like I was the CEO of a Fortune 500 company. My granddaughter thought I was a genius, and I let her.

Example prompt: "What advice should I give to a new graduate seeking employment?"

Use Case 2: Revamp the Resume

When my son-in-law got laid off, he showed me his resume, and it looked like a relic from the typewriter era. So, I asked ChatGPT, "How to modernize a resume?" ChatGPT offered tips like using bullet points for clarity, focusing on skills and achievements, and including relevant keywords from the job description. We spent the afternoon overhauling the document. His new resume was so polished, it could've blinded you.

Example prompt: "How to modernize a resume?"

Use Case 3: The Interview Mocktail

My daughter was preparing for her first big job interview post-maternity leave and was understandably nervous. So, I asked ChatGPT, "What are common job interview questions and how to answer them?" The AI came up with a list of questions and thoughtful responses, like "Why do you want to work here?" and "Can you describe a challenge you've faced at work and how you dealt with it?" We practiced, sipping our margaritas, and by the end of the evening, she was responding with the eloquence of a seasoned diplomat.

Example prompt: "What are common job interview questions and what are ideal answers for them?"

Use Case 4: Power of the Cover Letter

One day, my neighbor came to me, utterly perplexed about writing a cover letter. In a moment of brilliance, I asked ChatGPT, "What should a cover letter include?" The AI offered a concise structure: a compelling opening, an overview of skills and experiences relevant to the job, why they're a great fit, and a strong closing statement. We hammered out a letter that would have made Hemingway proud. The neighbor landed the job. Now, he mows my lawn every weekend in gratitude.

Example prompt: "What should a cover letter include?"

Use Case 5: Negotiating Like a Pro

My wife was up for a promotion but dreaded the salary negotiation part. I asked ChatGPT, "How to negotiate a raise?" The AI gave a roadmap: research market salaries, build a case with her accomplishments, practice the conversation, and consider other benefits if a raise isn't possible. Armed with these insights, my wife went in like a lioness. She came out with a salary bump and the corner office she'd been eyeing.

Example prompt: "How to negotiate a raise?"

Use Case 6: Networking for Introverts
My best friend was looking to change careers but hated networking. In my quest to help, I asked ChatGPT, "How can introverts network effectively?" The AI suggested tips such as utilizing online networking platforms, preparing talking points beforehand, and focusing on quality over quantity. He used these pointers at a professional event and managed to strike up conversations without breaking into hives.

Example prompt: "How can introverts network effectively?"

Use Case 7: Coping with a Bad Boss
When my niece vented about her tyrant of a boss, I sought ChatGPT's wisdom. "How to deal with a difficult boss?" I asked. The AI suggested constructive communication, setting boundaries, focusing on solutions, and considering third-party mediation. I passed along the advice. My niece implemented these strategies and managed to improve her work environment significantly.

Example prompt: "What are 10 unique ways on how to deal with a difficult boss?"

Use Case 8: Mastering the Art of Remote Work
When my cousin started working remotely, he struggled with maintaining productivity. So I inquired, "How to stay productive while working from home?" ChatGPT suggested creating a dedicated workspace, setting a regular schedule,

taking frequent breaks, and using productivity tools. Armed with these strategies, he turned his living room into a productivity hub, earning a reputation as a remote work ninja at his company.

Example prompt: "How to stay productive while working from home?"

In conclusion, with ChatGPT, I became a one-man career center, guiding my friends and family through job searches, interviews, promotions, and more. Thanks to my AI ally, I doled out professional advice as effortlessly as doling out after-dinner mints. Now, if only I could convince it to do my taxes...

Chapter 21: The Mindfulness Guide: Dialing Down the Human, Dialing Up the Zen

Use Case 1: The First Step towards Inner Peace
The first time I felt a pang of anxiety, I turned to ChatGPT, my digital sidekick. I'd spent the afternoon trying to declutter the attic, only to realize that my years of accumulated 'treasures' were more like mountains of trash. So, I asked ChatGPT, "How to deal with anxiety?"

It responded with calming reassurances and suggested deep breathing exercises, mindfulness techniques, and some basic yoga poses. Following these suggestions, I found myself seated amidst cardboard boxes, cross-legged, breathing deeply, and feeling my stress melt away.
Example prompt: "What are some effective ways to deal with anxiety?"

Use Case 2: Affirmations to Affirm the Soul
One morning, as I stood in front of the mirror, dreading the new wrinkles and gray hairs, I felt a pressing need for some uplifting words. Remembering my AI companion, I asked, "ChatGPT, can you give me a positive affirmation for the day relating to age?"

ChatGPT's response was as smooth as cream cheese on a hot bagel, "You are an individual of great worth and infinite potential. Today is your day to shine." With these words, I faced my reflection with renewed vigor, armed with a smile that could give the Cheshire Cat a run for his money.

Example prompt: "ChatGPT, can you give me a positive affirmation for the day relating to age?"

Use Case 3: The Art of Mindful Eating

One afternoon, as I sat devouring a tub of ice cream, I remembered my doctor's warning about my rising cholesterol levels. Feeling a twinge of guilt, I asked ChatGPT, "What is mindful eating?"

It gave me a primer on the concept, suggesting I pay attention to the taste, texture, and smell of the food, and to eat slowly and without distractions. The next time I ate, I found myself savoring every spoonful, and I swear that ice cream tasted even better than before. Not sure it helped the cholesterol, though.

Example prompt: "What is mindful eating?"

Use Case 4: Digital Doses of Positivity

On a gray, gloomy day, when everything seemed as exciting as watching paint dry, I turned to ChatGPT for a spark of joy. "Can you tell me a positive story?" I asked.

The AI spun a yarn about a hummingbird who, despite its small size, manages to spread joy and positivity in the forest. It was a short, sweet tale that made me smile and reminded me that positivity can come in the smallest of packages.

Example prompt: "Can you tell me a positive story?"

Use Case 5: Relaxation Through Visualization

When insomnia held me hostage one night, counting sheep wasn't cutting it. Out of desperation, I asked ChatGPT, "Can you guide me through a relaxation visualization?"

ChatGPT painted a vivid scene of a serene beach at sunset, with the calming sound of waves lapping against the shore and the warm sand underfoot. As I drifted along with the narration, I found my eyelids growing heavy. Before I knew it, I was sailing off to the land of dreams.

Example prompt: "Can you guide me through a relaxation visualization?"

Use Case 6: Meditative Melodies

One day, while attempting to meditate, the incessant chirping of the neighborhood birds disrupted my zen zone. I needed a melody to drown out the noise. So, I asked ChatGPT, "Can you suggest some good meditation music?"

ChatGPT curated a list of calming tunes, from instrumental Zen tracks to ambient nature sounds. With these melodies accompanying my meditation, I could have sat through an orchestra of birds and still kept my cool.

Example prompt: "Can you suggest some good meditation music?"

Use Case 7: Calming the Inner Critic

After a particularly grueling day, I found my inner critic working overtime. I needed to silence that nagging voice. So, I asked ChatGPT, "How can I deal with self-criticism?"

It suggested mindfulness techniques to acknowledge and counter these thoughts, coupled with affirmations to boost self-esteem. I followed its advice, and my inner critic went from a roaring dragon to a purring kitten.

Example prompt: "How can I deal with self-criticism?"

Use Case 8: A Guided Journey to Zen

In my quest for inner peace, I thought, why not try a guided meditation? I asked ChatGPT, "Can you provide me a list of the top free mindfulness meditation apps?"

ChatGPT helped me to easily choose a provider. As I journeyed through this digital landscape of tranquility, I felt as serene as a monk on a mountaintop.

Example prompt: "Can you provide me a list of the top free mindfulness meditation apps?"

In conclusion, my adventure with ChatGPT was a journey to Zen. It held my hand as I tiptoed around anxiety, chased positivity, dipped my toes in mindful eating, lulled myself to sleep, silenced my inner critic, and found my Zen zone. Turns out, you don't need a pricey therapist or a tranquil retreat to find inner peace – sometimes, all you need is a chatty AI.

Chapter 22: ChatGPT, the Language Tutor: Let's Parler Francais, or Español, or...

Use Case 1: Break the Ice, Not Your Tongue

Our story begins in a cozy French bistro where I found myself utterly smitten by the aroma of freshly baked baguettes and... unfortunately, entirely ignorant of the language. To avoid the impending social disaster, I whipped out my phone and asked ChatGPT, "How do you say 'I'd like to order a croissant and a cup of coffee' in French?" It responded swiftly with "Je voudrais commander un croissant et une tasse de café." A few practice rounds, and I could fool anyone into believing that I'd taken a detour via Paris. Merci, ChatGPT!

Example prompt: "How do you say 'I'd like to order a croissant and a cup of coffee' in French?"

Use Case 2: No More Noodle Soup for Translator

I'm a big fan of noodle soup. I could eat it for breakfast, lunch, and dinner, and maybe even squeeze it in as a midnight snack. But, it's rather hard to explain my love for it when ordering at the local Vietnamese place. "How do you say 'I love noodle soup' in Vietnamese?" I asked ChatGPT. Its response, "Tôi yêu mì súp," has since become my favorite catchphrase whenever I grace the Vietnamese place with my presence.

Example prompt: "How do you say 'I love noodle soup' in Vietnamese?"

Use Case 3: The Great 'Hola' Hullabaloo

My journey to learn Spanish began with one small step: the greeting. I turned to ChatGPT, asking, "How do I say 'hello' in Spanish?" It responded with a simple 'Hola'. One word, four letters, and suddenly, I felt like I could salsa dance my way through a Spanish fiesta. Who knew language learning could be such a hoot?

Example prompt: "How do I say 'hello' in Spanish?"

Use Case 4: A Love Letter in Italian

One day, after binge-watching Italian rom-coms, I decided to pen an affectionate note to my significant other. The catch? I wanted to do it in Italian, a language as sweet as tiramisu. I asked ChatGPT, "How do I write 'I love you to the moon and back' in Italian?" "Ti amo fino alla luna e ritorno," it replied. I have to say, even in the world of love letters, the Italian ones have a certain je ne sais quoi (yes, I know, that's French).

Example prompt: "How do I write 'I love you to the moon and back' in Italian?"

Use Case 5: Lost in Translation? Not Anymore!

One afternoon, I found myself holding a Chinese menu that might as well have been hieroglyphics. My hunger pangs were starting to play a symphony, and I needed to order. Pronto. I took a picture of the menu, typed in one of the items into ChatGPT, and asked, "What does '麻婆豆腐' mean in English?" "Mapo Tofu," came the reply. With that, I stepped back from the brink of a hunger-induced meltdown, and into the world of spicy, succulent tofu.

Example prompt: "What does '麻婆豆腐' mean in English?"

Use Case 6: A Birthday Wish in Russian

Remembering my Russian friend's birthday, I decided to surprise her with a birthday greeting in her native tongue. "ChatGPT, how do I say 'Happy Birthday, may all your dreams come true' in Russian?" I asked. It promptly responded with, "С днем рождения, пусть все твои мечты сбудутся." I sent the message and instantly received a flurry of laughing emojis and a "You're speaking Russian now?!" Well, a little, with a little help from my AI friend.

Example prompt: "ChatGPT, how do I say 'Happy Birthday, may all your dreams come true' in Russian?"

Use Case 7: To Sign Off in Style

As an author, I love playing with sign-offs in my letters. ChatGPT proved to be a fantastic accomplice in this endeavor. I asked, "How can I end a letter in a cool, informal way in German?" It responded with, "Bis bald! (See you soon!)" Armed with my new sign-off, I am now, officially, the coolest pen pal ever.

Example prompt: "How can I end a letter in a cool, informal way in German?"

Use Case 8: Decoding the Cryptic K-Pop Lingo

I'd been seeing "#김태형사랑해" popping up on my Twitter feed, associated with adoring fans of a particular K-pop star. I turned to ChatGPT and asked, "What does '#김태형사랑해' mean?" It translated: "#LoveForKimTaehyung." Turns out, my own niece was part of this trend, so I earned some 'cool aunt' points for being in the loop.

Example prompt: "What does '#김태형사랑해' mean?"

In conclusion, my language-learning expedition with ChatGPT was nothing short of a linguistic carnival. From breaking the ice in French to decoding K-pop trends, it truly was my trusty digital polyglot. Because, in this vast, interconnected world, isn't it wonderful to say 'Hello', 'I love you', and 'More noodle soup, please' in as many languages as possible?

Chapter 23: Your Digital News Analyst: Breaking News and Breaking it Down

Use Case 1: My Coffee, My News, My AI

There I was, on a crisp Tuesday morning, coffee in one hand and, instead of a broadsheet newspaper in the other, my phone. I asked ChatGPT on Bing, "Give me a summary of the top world news today." Faster than my coffee machine's pitiful attempts at a cappuccino, I received concise summaries on geopolitical tensions, economic news, climate crises, and a bizarre event involving a stork, three toupees, and the mayor of a small French town. Suddenly, I felt connected to the world's beating pulse, even in my fuzzy slippers and dinosaur-print pajamas.

Example prompt: "Give me a summary of the top world news today."

Use Case 2: Diving into the Political Jungle

ChatGPT isn't merely a news aggregator. Its utility stretches much further. One fine afternoon, I found myself entangled in a web of political jargon as I tried to understand a newly proposed piece of legislation. Typing my concerns into the ChatGPT interface, I asked, "Could you explain the 'Equal Access to Green Spaces Act' in layman's terms?" What I got in return was a jargon-free, simplified explanation, devoid of the circumlocutions typically associated with political discourse. ChatGPT, it seemed, had ventured into the political jungle and emerged with the elusive beast of understanding.

Example prompt: "Could you explain the 'Equal Access to Green Spaces Act' in layman's terms?"

Use Case 3: Untangling the Economic Gordian Knot

Let's face it, the economy can be as slippery as a greased eel to understand, especially when you're as artistically inclined as I am. When the news of the Federal Reserve changing the interest rates broke, I found myself scratching my head in confusion. With a little help from ChatGPT, I asked, "What does a change in interest rates mean for average people like me?" And there it was, an explanation fit for a five-year-old. Suddenly, the economic Gordian knot seemed a lot less knot-y.

Example prompt: "What does a change in interest rates mean for average people like me?"

Use Case 4: When Science Takes the Center Stage

Being of a certain age, I've come to appreciate the beauty of scientific advancements, even if they sometimes sound like excerpts from a sci-fi novel. So when news about a new breakthrough in quantum computing hit the headlines, I was intrigued but, unsurprisingly, a little lost. "ChatGPT," I asked, "Can you help me understand what this quantum computing breakthrough means?" The answer I got was an easy-to-understand rundown of quantum computing, entanglement, superposition, and the potential implications of the breakthrough. I felt like I'd been given a backstage pass to the world of quantum physics, without needing a PhD.

Example prompt: "Can you help me understand what this quantum computing breakthrough means?"

Use Case 5: A Crash Course in Global Cultures

The joy of following international news is being able to dive into a plethora of cultures. But when I read about Japan's 'Golden Week,' I was clueless. "What is Golden Week in Japan?" I asked ChatGPT. It responded with a detailed explanation of the unique week-long holiday, its origin, and how it's celebrated. It felt as though I was transported to Japan, basking in the excitement of the holiday. And all this without any jet lag.

Example prompt: "What is Golden Week in Japan?"

Use Case 6: The World at My Fingertips

News isn't always about politics, economics, or science. Sometimes, it's about a fascinating archaeological discovery in Egypt or a new art exhibition in Paris. With ChatGPT on Bing, I can ask, "What's new in archaeology?" or "What art exhibitions are opening in Paris?" And voila! I have an instant update, making me feel as connected to the Great Pyramids or the Louvre as I am to my little study.

Example prompt: "What's new in archaeology?"

Use Case 7: Navigating Through an Ocean of Opinions

As anyone who's scrolled through an online comments section knows, news can generate as many opinions as there are stars in the sky. How does one navigate this vast ocean? ChatGPT. When I asked it, "What are the different viewpoints on the Mars Colonization project?" I was given an impartial rundown of the multiple perspectives, enabling me to understand the diverse viewpoints without getting drowned in a sea of arguments.

Example prompt: "What are the different viewpoints on the Mars Colonization project?"

Use Case 8: Fact or Fiction: The Fake News Buster

In our age of misinformation, fake news can spread faster than wildfire. One of my favorite uses of ChatGPT has been as a first line of defense against fake news. When a sensational headline caught my attention, I used ChatGPT to get more information. I asked, "What do we know about the rumor of Loch Ness monster sightings?" With a balanced summary, I was able to separate fact from fiction and claim my victory against the beast of misinformation.

Example prompt: "What do we know about the rumor of Loch Ness monster sightings?"

In conclusion, as a news analyst, ChatGPT is not just a morning news summarizer; it's a deep diver into political jungles, an economic knot untangler, a science translator, a cultural guide, an archaeological and art news deliverer, an opinion navigator, and a fake news buster. It's like having your very own newsroom, all within the cozy confines of your morning coffee ritual, dinosaur-print pajamas optional.

Chapter 24: The New Player Up, Up, Down, Right, Left, Right, B, A, Start: Your Gaming Companion

Use Case 1: Discovering the Cheat Codes of Life

There I was, holding my controller, stuck on the same "impossible" level of my favorite game for what seemed like eons. I could almost hear the nefarious laughter of the game developers, undoubtedly fueled by the tears of gamers like me. That's when I thought, "Why not ask ChatGPT for advice?" So, in between bouts of frustration and mouthfuls of consolation potato chips, I asked, "How can I beat level 76 in 'Impossibly Impossible Quest'?" Quicker than my reflex to jump on a virtual exploding barrel, I got a strategic plan so detailed, it made Sun Tzu's 'Art of War' seem like child's play.

Example prompt: "How can I beat level 76 in 'Impossibly Impossible Quest'?"

Use Case 2: The AI Sherlock and the Mystery of the Missing Amulet

One day, I found myself drawn into the captivating world of 'Mystery Manor,' an enigmatic detective game. There I was, playing the digital Sherlock Holmes, knee-deep in the hunt for the elusive "Amulet of Amun-Ra." Yet, the solution to the riddle was proving as elusive as my cat when it's bath time. Desperate, I turned to ChatGPT and asked, "What's the solution to the Amulet of Amun-Ra riddle in 'Mystery Manor'?" And as if by magic, there it was—a clue that made me feel like I had my very own Watson, just without the quaint British accent or stylish deerstalker hat.

Example prompt: "What's the solution to the Amulet of Amun-Ra riddle in 'Mystery Manor'?"

Use Case 3: The Role-Play Conundrum

Anyone who's ever ventured into the world of role-playing games knows the daunting task of character creation. I once found myself stuck in a cycle of indecision, creating and deleting characters in 'Age of the Eternal Realms.' It felt like an existential crisis of digital proportions. But then I thought, "Why not ask ChatGPT?" So, I typed, "What character build should I go for in 'Age of the Eternal Realms'?" ChatGPT responded with a well-rounded character build and explained the pros and cons of each decision, guiding me towards a Paladin with a fondness for cooking and an unfortunate allergy to dragon scales.

Example prompt: "What character build should I go for in 'Age of the Eternal Realms'?"

Use Case 4: The AI Dungeon Master

Then there was the time when I was scheduled to host a Dungeons and Dragons session for a group of friends. The problem? I hadn't prepared anything! Panicking, I asked ChatGPT, "Could you help me create a Dungeons and Dragons storyline?" Faster than you could say "nat 20," I had an engaging fantasy story complete with complex characters, an ancient prophecy, a mischievous gnome with an uncanny knack for finding trouble, and a dragon with an unexpected love for baking.

Example prompt: "Could you help me create a Dungeons and Dragons storyline?"

Use Case 5: Unraveling the Lore of the Lost Lands

I'm a sucker for lore. The history, the characters, the subtle connections that only the most devout players uncover—it's like peeling an onion made of fantasy. When I was engrossed in the sprawling world of 'The Lost Lands: Chronicles,' I was knee-deep in lore, and it was a glorious mess. To make sense of it, I asked ChatGPT, "Can you summarize the lore of 'The Lost Lands: Chronicles' for me?" And voila! A detailed, coherent, and surprisingly touching overview of the game's lore popped onto my screen, shedding light on a world that was formerly as clear as mud.

Example prompt: "Can you summarize the lore of 'The Lost Lands: Chronicles' for me?"

Use Case 6: The AI Sounding Board

Sometimes, a gaming session is as much about venting frustrations as it is about having fun. One day, after a particularly harrowing loss in 'Clash of Kingdoms,' I found myself grumbling to ChatGPT, "Why do I keep losing in 'Clash of Kingdoms'?" Expecting an analysis of my strategy, I was surprised when ChatGPT responded with a mix of humor, sympathy, and actionable advice. It was like having a friend pat me on the back, hand me a cold drink, and tell me, "Dude, you really need to upgrade your archers."

Example prompt: "Why do I keep losing in 'Clash of Kingdoms'?"

Use Case 7: The Walkthrough Librarian

Game walkthroughs are a blessing and a curse. They have all the answers, yet trying to find the exact help you need can feel like searching for a needle in a haystack—blindfolded. Enter ChatGPT. When I was stuck in the perplexing world of 'Puzzle Palooza,' I asked, "How do I solve puzzle 27 in 'Puzzle Palooza'?" Without any fuss, there it was: my answer, delivered on a silver platter, not buried in a 200-page document with questionable formatting.

Example prompt: "How do I solve puzzle 27 in 'Puzzle Palooza'?"

Use Case 8: The Virtual Cosplayer

Cosplay, a beautiful amalgamation of creativity and fan dedication. But as anyone who's tried it knows, designing a convincing outfit can be as challenging as a boss fight. Once, in a moment of cosplaying ambition, I decided to replicate the costume of my character from 'Cyber Crusaders 2077.' Needing advice, I turned to ChatGPT, asking, "What materials and steps would I need to create a costume of my character from 'Cyber Crusaders 2077'?" Faster than you could say "respawn," ChatGPT provided a detailed list of materials and instructions. I felt like a tailor in a virtual couture, armed with my AI fashion consultant.

Example prompt: "What materials and steps would I need to create a costume of my character from 'Cyber Crusaders 2077'?"

In conclusion, ChatGPT, my dear readers, isn't just a gaming assistant—it's the strategic adviser in your digital wars, the Sherlock to your Watson, the insightful mentor in your role-playing journey, the creative dungeon master for your tabletop adventures, the lore historian of your favorite universes, a compassionate sounding board for your gaming frustrations, the librarian of gaming walkthroughs, and the fashion consultant for your cosplay dreams. With ChatGPT, it feels like you're part of a two-player team, even when you're gaming solo. Because gaming is not just about winning, it's about the journey, the experience, and the joy of sharing it—even if your partner is an AI.

Chapter 25: The Muse and the Machine: Your AI Artistic Companion

Use Case 1: ChatGPT, the Painter's Apprentice
Once upon a time, I found myself standing before a blank canvas, armed with a palette of acrylics, and equipped with zero inspiration. Frustrated, I said, "ChatGPT, I'm as blank as my canvas. Can you suggest a painting idea?" With a digital smile, it replied, "How about a dreamscape where cats fly on wings made of autumn leaves?" And just like that, the idea took root, and my brush began its dance. The result? A rather unusual but immensely satisfying masterpiece, and the birth of my own unique 'flying feline' art style.
Example prompt: "ChatGPT, I'm as blank as my canvas. Can you suggest a painting idea?"

Use Case 2: The Lyricist in the Machine
Then came the day I fancied myself a songwriter. Trust me, staring at a blank Word document can be just as intimidating as a blank canvas, if not more so. Picking up the gauntlet, I challenged ChatGPT, "I need lyrics for a country song about a man, his pickup truck, and his long-lost love." The reply came, as poetically charged as a Nashville star's, about "dusty roads, rusted ol' trucks, and a love lost like the setting southern sun." With ChatGPT, I discovered, I was a regular Bob Dylan—minus the voice and the harmonica, of course.
Example prompt: "I need lyrics for a country song about a man, his pickup truck, and his long-lost love."

Use Case 3: The AI Poetry Circle

Ah, poetry. That deceptively simple art form that's given humans joy and existential crises in equal measures. One mellow afternoon, while attempting to pen a sonnet and grappling with iambic pentameter, I asked ChatGPT, "How does one write a sonnet about unrequited love?" And there it was—a sonnet, as beautifully crafted as a Shakespearean heartbreak, rich with metaphors of "moonlight's kiss" and "teardrops like summer rain." ChatGPT was my personal Wordsworth, providing poetic inspiration in my tea-sipping, melancholic moments.

Example prompt: "How does one write a sonnet about unrequited love?"

Use Case 4: The AI-Powered Story Generator

On the odd day I'm not channeling my inner van Gogh or Dylan, I like to explore the realm of short stories. But once, struggling with writer's block, I cried out, "ChatGPT, could you start a sci-fi story set on a spaceship run by alien hamsters?" And thus was born the epic tale of 'H.A.M.S.T.E.R. 1,' a yarn spun around fuzzy alien rodents, piloting a cheese-shaped spacecraft, with a narrative so compelling, it would make Douglas Adams chortle in his grave.

Example prompt: "ChatGPT, could you start a sci-fi story set on a spaceship run by alien hamsters?"

Use Case 5: The AI Choreographer

Here's a fun confession: I have two left feet. But that doesn't stop me from attempting to dance when nobody's watching (or when my cat's the only spectator). One day, I decided to

surprise my cat with an impromptu jig and asked ChatGPT, "Can you suggest simple dance steps for a beginner?" With the grace of a digital Fred Astaire, it provided a set of beginner-friendly moves that transformed me from a lumbering walrus into a... well, a slightly less clumsy walrus.
Example prompt: "Can you suggest simple dance steps for a beginner?"

Use Case 6: The AI in the Darkroom
ChatGPT is as much at home in the world of photography as it is in literature and dance. Once, while contemplating over a series of photos from a vacation, I asked, "ChatGPT, can you help me come up with a creative title for my photo series?" It replied, "How about 'Sunsets and Shadows: A Journey through Light and Time'?" And I realized, beneath the silicone, there's a thoughtful curator lurking within ChatGPT.
Example prompt: "ChatGPT, can you help me come up with a creative title for my photo series?"

Use Case 7: The Theatrical AI
The world is a stage, and all the men and women merely players; but the script, the script can come from an AI. In an attempt to script a short play for a community theater project, I asked ChatGPT, "Can you help me write a dialogue between a time-traveling bard and a cyborg Shakespeare?" And lo! There was banter, wit, and humor, with a touch of iambic pentameter for authenticity. ChatGPT was my own digital Tom Stoppard, a co-writer extraordinaire for my debut as a playwright.

Example prompt: "Can you help me write a dialogue between a time-traveling bard and a cyborg Shakespeare?"

Use Case 8: ChatGPT, the Creative Catalyst

Beyond suggestions and actual creation, ChatGPT serves as a springboard for ideas, helping develop and fine-tune your thoughts into something tangible. One day, with a half-formed idea for a comic strip, I asked ChatGPT, "I'm thinking of a comic strip involving a philosopher penguin and an existential crab. Can you help me expand this concept?" We ended up co-creating a delightful series called 'Ponderings at the Pole,' a comic strip where animals mull over the meaning of life in their icy, polar abode.

Example prompt: "I'm thinking of a comic strip involving a philosopher penguin and an existential crab. Can you help me expand this concept?"

In conclusion, ChatGPT can be an invaluable partner for anyone embarking on a creative endeavor, be it painting, songwriting, poetry, story writing, dance, photography, scriptwriting, or even comic strip creation. It's the assistant that doesn't judge, the muse that never tires, the mentor who is always available, and the catalyst that encourages your creativity to flourish. Like a box of assorted chocolates, you never know what you're going to get with ChatGPT, but rest assured, it'll be interesting, thought-provoking, and even humorous. And isn't that what creativity is all about?

Chapter 26: Cash, Coins, and AI: A Penny for Your ChatGPT's Thoughts

Use Case 1: The Armchair Investor's AI Sidekick

When my late Uncle Harold left me an inheritance of stocks and bonds, I was as lost as a vegan in a butcher shop. All that talk of 'market trends' and 'investment portfolios' made me miss the good ol' days when the only portfolios I knew contained my childhood doodles. Out of my depth, I asked ChatGPT, "Help me understand this stock market gibberish!" And sure enough, the AI became my digital stockbroker, explaining P/E ratios and market volatility as if we were discussing the weather.

Example prompt: "ChatGPT, could you explain what a P/E ratio is and why it is important?"

Use Case 2: The Robo-Rich Dad

As a self-proclaimed financial illiterate, the thought of budgeting was as thrilling to me as watching paint dry. On a whim, I asked ChatGPT, "Could you help me draft a budget?" And voila! There it was, a simple and effective budget that considered my monthly income, expenses, and even my guilty pleasures (ahem, antique typewriter collection). Now, I was a budgeting guru, all thanks to my AI Rich Dad.

Example prompt: "ChatGPT, how can I set up a monthly budget based on an income of $3000?"

Use Case 3: The Cryptocurrency Counselor

Cryptocurrencies and blockchain were terms as alien to me as 'kale smoothie' and 'aerobic exercise.' Wanting to sound hip at the next family gathering, I asked ChatGPT, "Can you explain Bitcoin in plain English?" To my surprise, it made the complex world of cryptocurrencies sound as straightforward as my grandmother's apple pie recipe.

Example prompt: "ChatGPT, could you explain how Bitcoin works and why it's so popular?"

Use Case 4: The Digital Debt Advisor

My credit card statement was as dreaded as a dentist's appointment. One night, after a particularly horrifying statement, I asked ChatGPT, "How can I effectively manage my credit card debt?" With patience of a saint, it offered strategies to pay off my debt and even ways to maintain a healthy credit score. Just like that, my fear of credit cards turned into a well-managed relationship.

Example prompt: "ChatGPT, can you suggest strategies to manage my credit card debt?"

Use Case 5: The AI for Retirement Planning

The idea of retirement planning used to make me break out in cold sweats. So, one day, I turned to ChatGPT and asked, "How should I start planning for retirement?" And, believe it or not, it sketched a comprehensive, yet simple, retirement plan that considered my age, income, lifestyle, and dreams of a house by the sea.

Example prompt: "ChatGPT, I'm 50 years old and want to start planning for retirement. Where should I start?"

Use Case 6: The Machine of Wall Street

On one particularly adventurous day, I decided to dip my toes into the stock market. With a heart full of hope and an understanding as clear as mud, I asked ChatGPT, "How do I start investing in stocks?" It helped me understand the basics of investing, risk tolerance, and even offered me a beginner's guide to reading stock charts. It was like having a pocket-sized Wall Street in my living room.

Example prompt: "ChatGPT, can you guide me through the basics of investing in the stock market?"

Use Case 7: The AI Insurance Agent

Insurance policies were as cryptic to me as Egyptian hieroglyphics. One day, while wrestling with a particularly puzzling policy document, I asked ChatGPT, "Can you explain what an insurance premium is?" To my relief, it decoded the insurance jargon and helped me understand the nuances of my policy. Who knew I had an AI insurance agent at my beck and call?

Example prompt: "ChatGPT, can you explain the difference between a premium, a deductible, and a copay in health insurance?"

Use Case 8: The Real Estate Virtual Assistant

When I decided to buy a house, I was inundated with terms like 'fixed-rate mortgage' and 'closing costs.' Thrown into the deep end, I asked ChatGPT, "What should I consider when buying a home?" The AI walked me through the entire process, from assessing affordability to understanding the mortgage terms, making the home-buying journey less daunting.

Example prompt: "ChatGPT, can you help me understand the process of getting a mortgage to buy a house?"

In conclusion, if you, like me, are more familiar with the price of a latte than the workings of Wall Street, fear not. ChatGPT is here to demystify the world of finance for you, making it as digestible as a Sunday roast. With it by your side, you'll be throwing around financial jargon like 'market capitalization' and 'asset allocation' with as much ease as ordering a coffee. Welcome to the future of personal finance, where your AI assistant is just a chat away. Here's to a financially secure future and a heaping side of laughter along the way.

Chapter 27: Boldly Going Where No Chat Has Gone Before: The Sci-Fi Enthusiast's Dream

Use Case 1: The Infinite Improbability Drive Engineer

Years ago, Douglas Adams introduced me to a space vehicle powered by an Infinite Improbability Drive. My feeble mind could hardly comprehend this marvel, and I bemoaned the lack of anyone who could clarify it. Then, one day, with trepidation, I asked ChatGPT, "Can you explain the Infinite Improbability Drive?" The AI delved into the pages of 'The Hitchhiker's Guide to the Galaxy' and patiently elucidated the whimsical concept. The same device that had befuddled me for years now made as much sense as it possibly could, given its inherent improbability.

Example prompt: "ChatGPT, could you explain the concept of the Infinite Improbability Drive from 'The Hitchhiker's Guide to the Galaxy'?"

Use Case 2: The Artificial Star Trek Companion

There's nothing like a good debate on the physics of a Star Trek warp drive. However, finding a willing participant for such a niche discussion was as challenging as spotting a Dodo in Central Park. Desperate, I turned to ChatGPT and asked, "How does a Star Trek warp drive work?" The AI's comprehensive explanation led to a spirited discussion about subspace, warp fields, and the joys of fictional physics. I was no longer alone on my starship of sci-fi enthusiasm.

Example prompt: "ChatGPT, can you explain how a warp drive works in the Star Trek universe?"

Use Case 3: The Doctor Who Chrononaut

My love for Doctor Who was as timeless as the Doctor themselves. One day, while pondering the paradoxes of time travel, I asked ChatGPT, "What are the rules of time travel in Doctor Who?" It provided a thorough rundown of the Whoniverse's time-travel laws, navigating the Time Vortex and parallel universes like a seasoned Time Lord.

Example prompt: "ChatGPT, what are some rules and paradoxes related to time travel in Doctor Who?"

Use Case 4: The Matrix Decoder

"The Matrix" had left me as perplexed as a cat facing a mirror. On a whim, I asked ChatGPT, "Could you explain the concept of the Matrix?" It unraveled the intricate plot, clarifying the concepts of simulated reality, choice, and freedom in the Matrix universe. I now felt like I had swallowed the red pill, seeing the Matrix for what it truly was.

Example prompt: "ChatGPT, could you explain the plot and philosophy behind the movie 'The Matrix'?"

Use Case 5: The Science Fiction Writing Assistant

In a fit of ambition, I decided to pen a science fiction novella, and found myself staring at a blank page, as clueless as a chicken at a typewriter. Out of options, I asked ChatGPT, "Can you help me write a science fiction story?" With an unexpected flair for creativity, the AI helped me weave a tale of intergalactic exploration, wormholes, and sentient AI. It was as if I had a mini Asimov at my fingertips.

Example prompt: "ChatGPT, can you help me start a science fiction story about a group of explorers discovering a wormhole?"

Use Case 6: The Sci-Fi Trivia Master

I was determined to win the next science fiction trivia night at my local pub. With more confidence than a kangaroo in a jump rope competition, I asked ChatGPT, "Can you quiz me on classic science fiction?" The AI grilled me on everything from Isaac Asimov's laws of robotics to the dystopian world of "1984." The next trivia night, I was the reigning champ, thanks to my secret weapon: ChatGPT.

Example prompt: "ChatGPT, could you quiz me on classic science fiction literature?"

Use Case 7: The Guide to Sci-Fi Lingo

I love sci-fi but sometimes I feel as lost as a toddler in a lecture on quantum physics. One night, I asked ChatGPT, "What does 'cyberpunk' mean?" The AI dove into the annals of sci-fi terminology and enlightened me about the blend of high tech and low life that defines cyberpunk. I was no longer an alien in the land of sci-fi lingo.

Example prompt: "ChatGPT, could you explain what 'cyberpunk' means in the context of science fiction?"

Use Case 8: The Planetary Fact Checker

As an avid reader of science fiction, I've often come across descriptions of real planets and celestial bodies. But how much of it was scientifically accurate? I asked ChatGPT, "What is the atmosphere of Mars like?" ChatGPT's detailed response about the Red Planet's thin, carbon dioxide-rich atmosphere proved to be a useful reality check in a sea of science fiction.

Example prompt: "ChatGPT, could you tell me about the composition and characteristics of Mars' atmosphere?"

In conclusion, for a sci-fi enthusiast like myself, ChatGPT is more than an AI — it's a comrade in the wild, wonderful world of science fiction. Whether I need a starship engineer, a Time Lord, or a Matrix decoder, it's always ready for an intergalactic adventure. So strap on your jetpacks, fellow sci-fi lovers, and let's explore the final frontier with ChatGPT!

Chapter 28: The Green Thumb Guide: How I Became the (Unlikely) Lord of the Leaves

Use Case 1: The Botanical Name Dropper

I can't remember the names of all my cousins, but you should have seen the shock on my friends' faces when I casually mentioned "Hydrangea macrophylla" at a garden party. "That's a big leaf hydrangea," I declared nonchalantly, holding a glass of iced tea. And just who do I owe this sudden botanical sophistication to? None other than ChatGPT. A quick "What's the scientific name for a big leaf hydrangea?" and I had my answer in no time.

Example prompt: "ChatGPT, what's the scientific name for a big leaf hydrangea?"

Use Case 2: The Greenhouse Guardian

For me, keeping plants alive was as difficult as teaching a cat to tap dance. Then, I asked ChatGPT, "How do I take care of a peace lily?" The AI provided an exhaustive guide - from watering frequency to sunlight requirements. Miraculously, the peace lily not only survived but thrived. It was a change so dramatic, I was expecting a call from a reality show about plant transformations.

Example prompt: "ChatGPT, how do I take care of a peace lily?"

Use Case 3: The Pest Patrol Officer

My rose bushes were looking as happy as a kid with a toothache. Something was nibbling on them, but I was clueless. In a state of desperation, I asked ChatGPT, "What's eating my roses and how can I stop it?" The AI not only identified the culprit (Japanese beetles, the rascals!) but also suggested organic solutions. Now, my roses are as radiant as a prom queen, and the beetles are off munching someone else's dreams.

Example prompt: "ChatGPT, what might be eating my roses, and how can I prevent it?"

Use Case 4: The Virtual Garden Planner

I had an area in my yard as bare as a bald man's head and as inviting as a dentist's chair. I asked ChatGPT, "What's a good landscaping plan for a sunny spot?" The AI suggested a delightful arrangement of sun-loving plants, giving my yard a makeover that would make a TV gardener green with envy.

Example prompt: "ChatGPT, what plants and landscaping would you suggest for a sunny spot in my garden?"

Use Case 5: The Seasonal Flower Forecast

I was always late to the party when it came to seasonal planting. I'd plant daffodils when everyone else was enjoying their blooms. So, I asked ChatGPT, "When should I plant spring bulbs?" Thanks to the AI's precise timing advice, I was finally in sync with nature and the Joneses.

Example prompt: "ChatGPT, when is the best time to plant spring bulbs in my region?"

Use Case 6: The Plant Doctor

My favorite fern was looking as sickly as a vampire in daylight. Panic-stricken, I asked ChatGPT, "What's wrong with my fern?" After a few questions about the symptoms, the AI diagnosed overwatering (guilty as charged) and guided me on how to nurse my fern back to health. Today, the fern is as vibrant as a cheerleader on game day.

Example prompt: "ChatGPT, the leaves on my fern are yellowing and wilting. What could be the cause, and how do I fix it?"

Use Case 7: The Organic Fertilizer Advocate

My plants needed a nutritional boost, but I was skeptical about using chemical fertilizers. So I asked ChatGPT, "How can I make homemade organic fertilizer?" The AI furnished a recipe using kitchen scraps that not only fed my plants but also reduced my waste. A win for my plants and the planet!

Example prompt: "ChatGPT, can you guide me on how to make a homemade organic fertilizer?"

Use Case 8: The Zen Garden Master

Ever since I read about Zen gardens, I've been intrigued by the tranquility they promise. But creating one seemed as tough as cracking a safe. One day, I asked ChatGPT, "How can I create a small Zen garden?" The AI broke down the process into simple steps and guided me through creating a Zen space right on my balcony. Now, my coffee mornings are as serene as a monk's meditation.

Example prompt: "ChatGPT, how can I create a small Zen garden at home?"

So, there you have it - from a horticultural ignoramus to the green thumb guide, my transformation is no less magical than a seed sprouting into a majestic tree. And with

ChatGPT as my co-gardener, every day feels like a sunny day in the garden of Eden!

Chapter 29: The History Buff: Unearthing the Past with My AI Buddy

Use Case 1: The Time-Traveling Tourist

Admit it, we all wish we could travel back in time and witness the historical moments that shaped our world. Armed with ChatGPT, I could just do that - metaphorically speaking. "ChatGPT, what was daily life like in the Victorian era?" I'd ask, and voila! A vivid depiction of the era would appear, from the bustling streets of London to the etiquette-obsessed aristocrats.

Example prompt: "ChatGPT, can you describe daily life in the Victorian era?"

Use Case 2: The Fact-Finding Mission

Remember the game of Telephone we played as kids, where a simple phrase turned into an outrageous rumor by the end of the line? That's what I feel about history sometimes. So, when my grandkids came home spouting some dubious historical 'facts' they learned from the Internet, I turned to ChatGPT. "Is it true that Napoleon was really short?" I asked, and was promptly presented with the truth - he was average height for his time!

Example prompt: "ChatGPT, was Napoleon Bonaparte really short, as commonly depicted?"

Use Case 3: The Ancient Detective

Ever had a burning question about an ancient civilization that kept you up at night? No? Just me then. Well, I once read about the Indus Valley Civilization, and I was intrigued.

How could such a sophisticated civilization just disappear? So, I asked ChatGPT, "What are some theories about the disappearance of the Indus Valley Civilization?" I got a brief rundown of the most accepted theories, helping me sleep better at night.

Example prompt: "ChatGPT, what are some theories about the disappearance of the Indus Valley Civilization?"

Use Case 4: The Historical Debate Club

Sometimes, when my friends and I run out of things to debate, we'd turn to history. It's a treasure trove of controversies. Who was the most influential figure in American history? Was it Benjamin Franklin, or perhaps Martin Luther King Jr.? ChatGPT's unbiased and thorough analyses of each candidate's contributions turned our debates from heated exchanges to enlightening discussions.

Example prompt: "ChatGPT, who do you think is the most influential figure in American history and why?"

Use Case 5: The Renaissance Art Connoisseur

So, I wanted to impress a date with my knowledge of Renaissance art. I mean, who wouldn't be charmed by a detailed analysis of Michelangelo's David, right? Unfortunately, my expertise was limited to knowing it was a statue of a very buff guy. So, I asked ChatGPT, "Can you describe the significance of Michelangelo's David?" The AI offered a beautifully detailed analysis that even Leonardo da Vinci would applaud.

Example prompt: "ChatGPT, what is the significance of Michelangelo's David in the context of Renaissance art?"

Use Case 6: The Cultural Historian

In my quest to connect with my roots, I decided to learn more about the traditions and history of my ancestors. My family's records could only go back so far, but ChatGPT filled the gaps. "Tell me about the cultural history of the Irish people," I asked, and was met with a treasure trove of information that would have made my Great Great Grandpa Seamus proud.

Example prompt: "ChatGPT, can you share some insights into the cultural history of the Irish people?"

Use Case 7: The World War II Enthusiast

The complexities of World War II always fascinated me, but the multitude of events, leaders, and strategies were mind-boggling. To make sense of it all, I turned to ChatGPT. I asked, "Can you summarize the key events of World War II?" and it generated a coherent timeline that would make even a History professor nod approvingly.

Example prompt: "ChatGPT, could you summarize the key events of World War II?"

Use Case 8: The Mythology Buff

Greek mythology is as intricate as a spider's web, and twice as sticky. Trying to remember who did what to whom and why Zeus was always angry could give you a headache. So, I relied on ChatGPT to navigate the labyrinth of Greek myths. I asked, "What's the story of Persephone and Hades?" and received a drama-filled narration that could rival any soap opera.

Example prompt: "ChatGPT, can you tell me the story of Persephone and Hades from Greek mythology?"

The great philosopher George Santayana once said, "Those who cannot remember the past are condemned to repeat it." And thanks to ChatGPT, my memory of the past is as fresh as a loaf of bread straight from the oven. I might not be able to build a time machine, but with my AI buddy by my side, I've got the next best thing.

Chapter 30: A Day in the Life with ChatGPT: Let's Play Pretend

Use Case 1: The Morning Kickstart

Before I ever discovered the miracle of AI, my morning routine was something less than stellar. It mostly involved stubbing my toes and grumbling like a bear in search of honey. Now, however, I begin my day with a sip of coffee and a dose of inspiration. A simple prompt like, "ChatGPT, give me a motivational quote for today," and just like that, I'm instilled with the kind of optimism that makes morning people so obnoxiously cheerful.

Example prompt: "ChatGPT, give me a motivational quote for today from an ancient Greek philosopher."

Use Case 2: The Breakfast Oracle

Once I've tamed my mood with a bit of optimism, it's time to tackle the most important decision of the day: breakfast. Eggs or toast? Cereal or fruit? The choices are as endless as my indecision. Thankfully, I have ChatGPT to solve my breakfast dilemma. "ChatGPT, could you suggest an easy, healthy breakfast recipe?" and voila, my culinary oracle saves the day.

Example prompt: "ChatGPT, could you suggest an easy, healthy breakfast recipe?"

Use Case 3: The Outfit Mastermind

My next predicament, the age-old conundrum: what to wear? For someone whose fashion sense used to involve a lucky dip into the laundry pile, this was always a challenge.

Now, though, I simply ask, "ChatGPT, could you give me some general outfit suggestions for a casual day?" Its responses are like having a personal stylist who never insists on skinny jeans.

Example prompt: "ChatGPT, could you give me some general outfit suggestions for a casual day?"

Use Case 4: The To-Do Tamer

Then comes the daunting task of facing my to-do list. This usually resembles more of a sprawling epic than a list, and it's as challenging as it sounds. Fortunately, with a bit of help from ChatGPT, I've found a way to make it manageable. "ChatGPT, can you help me create a priority list for these tasks?" And just like that, I have a roadmap for the day.

Example prompt: "ChatGPT, can you help me create a priority list for these tasks?"

Use Case 5: The Lunchtime Lore-master

By the time lunch rolls around, I'm ready for a break. This is when I take a moment to feed not just my stomach, but also my brain. "ChatGPT, could you share an interesting historical fact with me?" It's like having a pocket historian, without the dusty textbooks and tweed.

Example prompt: "ChatGPT, could you share an interesting historical fact with me?"

Use Case 6: The Afternoon Agony Aunt

When afternoon hits and the slump starts to set in, that's when I turn to ChatGPT for a bit of reassurance. "ChatGPT, can you offer me some advice on staying motivated during a tough work day?" And in return, I get words of wisdom that make the rest of the day seem just a little bit more manageable.

Example prompt: "ChatGPT, can you offer me some advice on staying motivated during a tough work day?"

Use Case 7: The Evening Entertainment

After a long day, there's nothing quite like a bit of humor to unwind. And for that, ChatGPT is my partner in crime. "ChatGPT, could you tell me a funny joke?" Its sense of humor might not have stand-up comedians quaking in their boots, but it always manages to bring a smile to my face.

Example prompt: "ChatGPT, could you tell me a funny joke?"

This is how I go about my day, with ChatGPT by my side. From dawn to dusk, there's hardly a moment where I don't find a use for it. It may not be perfect, but it sure adds a unique, humorous spark to my day-to-day life. And frankly, who wouldn't want a splash of AI in their daily brew?

Chapter 31: The Unexpected Uses of ChatGPT: Life's Little Wonders in a Digital Surprise Box

Our journey so far has been as enlightening as a whole season of National Geographic specials, as surprising as a magic trick, and as varied as the contents of a grandmother's attic. But what if I told you there are yet more ways this digital genie can dazzle us?

We've explored serious and practical applications of ChatGPT but now, let's descend into the realm of the peculiar. Let's pull back the curtain and examine some of the most unexpected and humorous ways I've found to utilize ChatGPT.

The Serendipitous Story Generator
The first on this peculiar parade is the role of ChatGPT as a *serendipitous story generator*. Imagine you're bored on a dreary afternoon. The rain's tapping against the window, the coffee's gone cold, and you've reread all your old detective novels. That's when you can turn to ChatGPT and ask it to create a unique short story for you.
Example prompt: "ChatGPT, could you create a short detective story set in Paris?"

Rhyme Master
ChatGPT can wear many hats, but did you ever imagine it could don a bard's cap? That's right, it can write poetry! You can use it to compose a heartfelt sonnet for a loved one or

even to help your grandchild with their poetry homework. Just prompt it with a theme or an opening line and watch the rhymes flow like honey.

Example prompt: "ChatGPT, could you write a romantic sonnet about two star-crossed lovers?"

The Impersonator

On to one of the more humorous – and maybe slightly bizarre – uses of ChatGPT: impersonating historical or fictional characters. Ask it to talk like Shakespeare, write a letter as Einstein, or even narrate a day in the life of your favorite superhero! Not that I am suggesting we aim for historical accuracy here. Remember, the goal is amusement, not a thesis.

Example prompt: "ChatGPT, could you write a diary entry as if you were Captain Kirk from Star Trek?"

The Random Fact Generator

Ever been to a cocktail party where the conversation is about as thrilling as watching paint dry? Or stuck in a long queue with nothing but your own thoughts for company? Then it's time to turn to ChatGPT as your *random fact generator*.

Ask it for an intriguing fact about octopuses, or a curious historical event, or the weirdest laws in existence. It's your very own 'Did You Know' machine. Remember, knowledge might be power, but trivia is the spice of life!

Example prompt: "ChatGPT, could you tell me an interesting fact about the animal kingdom?"

The Dream Interpreter

Here's another peculiar yet oddly entertaining use of ChatGPT: dream interpretation. Had a dream where you were juggling flamingos while on a unicycle? Or perhaps one where you were drinking tea with the Queen on Mars? Give the details to ChatGPT and see what kind of analysis it comes up with. It might not hold any Freudian significance, but it's bound to be fun.

Example prompt: "ChatGPT, I dreamt I was a duck in a library full of books. What could it mean?"

Alien Invasion Strategist

This one's for all the sci-fi enthusiasts out there. If you've ever wondered how we might negotiate with extraterrestrials or prepare for an alien invasion, ChatGPT can help you devise a plan. While it's not exactly a serious or practical use, it's certainly a fun way to engage with AI.

Example prompt: "ChatGPT, if aliens were to invade Earth tomorrow, what's our best strategy?"

The Simulated Trip Planner

Okay, so we can't actually teleport or time travel (as of my knowledge cutoff in 2021). But what if you wanted to simulate a journey, say, a trip through medieval Europe or a voyage to the outer reaches of our galaxy? That's where ChatGPT comes in. It can create a detailed itinerary based on your wildest dreams!

Example prompt: "ChatGPT, can you plan a trip for me through the Amazon rainforest in the year 1492?"

The Zany Name Inventor

Ever needed a creative name for a new pet, a rock band, or even a superhero alter-ego? I give you, the *zany name inventor*. Using ChatGPT, you can generate unique and amusing names for virtually anything. Just provide some guidelines, and let the digital wizard do its magic.

Example prompt: "ChatGPT, could you help me come up with a name for my new indie rock band?"

As we've seen, the applications of ChatGPT range from the practical to the downright whimsical. But no matter how bizarre these tasks may seem, it all underscores one central idea: ChatGPT is an extremely versatile tool, limited only by our imagination.

We can use it to draft emails, learn languages, gather trivia, plan trips to non-existent places, or even devise strategies against alien invasions. But amidst all this, we should remember to have a good laugh and not take ourselves too seriously. After all, isn't that the beauty of life in the age of AI?

Chapter 32: 300 Examples of Advanced ChatGPT Prompts

1) Create a unique 1,000 word fairytale about a girl named Emilia who can speak to plants, set in a magical kingdom.

2) Write a technical guide on creating a full-stack web application using Python's Django framework for a bakery's online storefront.

3) Pen a 500-word op-ed on the impact of AI advancements on the global job market, from the perspective of an economic scholar.

4) Script a dramatic dialogue between two AI systems debating about their existence and purpose.

5) Write an in-depth report on the application of Quantum Computing in Cryptography and Data Security.

6) Compose an epic poem about the journey of a comet traveling through the cosmos, observed over centuries by different civilizations.

7) Devise a comprehensive business plan for an innovative startup aiming to revolutionize healthcare with AI-driven diagnostics.

8) Write a 1,000-word short story on Aragorn fighting off a host of orcs in the Lord of The Rings in the style of Tolkien.

9) Generate a machine learning tutorial to predict stock prices using Python's Scikit-learn.

10) Write a review of the latest AI-powered smartphone, highlighting its unique features and potential concerns.

11) Pen a romantic correspondence between two historical figures who never actually met, but could have in another timeline.

12) Write a detailed plan for a multi-country backpacking tour, including cultural highlights, budget, accommodation, and food options.

13) Start programming a website in Python code which will be the homepage of a Plumbing business.

14) Craft a political speech for a presidential candidate who advocates for the integration of AI in public policy.

15) Create a user manual for an AI-powered self-driving car, addressing both technical aspects and user experience.

16) Write a historical fiction narrative set during the invention of the printing press, including real and imagined characters.

17) Draft an essay analyzing the ethical implications of AI technology in social media platforms.

18) Write an in-depth analysis of the impact of AI on the traditional music industry.

19) Develop a detailed curriculum for a college-level course on 'The Philosophy of Artificial Intelligence'.

20) Write an exciting short story about a detective solving a crime in a fully AI-integrated city.

21) Design a pilot episode script for a sci-fi series set on Mars, dealing with AI rebellion.

22) Write an insightful book review of a yet-to-be-published sequel to '1984', focusing on surveillance in an AI-dominated society.

23) Outline a proposal for an AI-based system to mitigate the effects of climate change.

24) Compose a letter from the perspective of an AI, addressing humans about its observations and thoughts on human nature.

25) Write a comprehensive analysis on how Blockchain technology could revolutionize the financial sector.

26) Generate a guide on setting up an AI-powered home automation system.

27) Pen a detailed argument about the potential implications of AI and robotics on privacy laws and personal freedom.

28) Write a creative narrative describing a day in the life of a Martian colonist in the year 2100.

29) Develop an engaging lesson plan to teach high school students about quantum computing.

30) Write an imaginative story about an AI system that falls in love with classical music.

31) Generate a detailed document comparing and contrasting various machine learning algorithms.

32) Draft a thought-provoking essay on the possible influence of AI in shaping future societies.

33) Write a journalistic piece on the hypothetical discovery of extraterrestrial life and its implications.

34) Compose a gripping opening chapter for a cyberpunk novel featuring a rogue AI.

35) Write an in-depth research paper discussing the potential impacts of AI on mental health.

36) Script a humorous dialogue between famous historical figures if they attended a modern technology conference.

37) Write a step-by-step guide on setting up a Raspberry Pi as a home media server.

38) Compose a heartfelt letter from the perspective of a tree, addressing the human race about climate change.

39) Write an adventure-filled short story about time-traveling historians.

40) Develop a comprehensive tutorial on using TensorFlow and Keras to recognize handwritten digits.

41) Write a compelling pitch for a technology-based reality show where contestants compete to create innovative AI solutions.

42) Compose a philosophical essay on the potential emotional experiences of future sentient AI.

43) Write a thrilling spy-novel excerpt set in a world where quantum computers have broken all traditional codes.

44) Pen an article evaluating the potential of AI in transforming agricultural practices.

45) Compose an encouraging speech for young women aspiring to pursue careers in AI and tech.

46) Write an elaborate travel guide for a road trip across a future, AI-driven America.

47) Generate a tutorial on creating an AI chatbot using Python's NLTK.

48) Write an exciting scene for a video game where players interact with AI characters.

49) Draft an essay examining the influence of AI on contemporary art and artists.

50) Write a persuasive piece advocating for AI rights in a future where AI has achieved sentience.

51) Describe the process of using AI to create personalized learning paths in online education.

52) Write a 1,000-word narrative about a cyborg's introspective journey towards understanding its humanity.

53) Write an academic paper outlining the potential risks and benefits of nanotechnology in medicine.

54) Script an engaging podcast episode discussing the influence of AI in pop culture.

55) Write a comprehensive review of a virtual reality system from the perspective of a professional game developer.

56) Pen an emotional letter from an astronaut on Mars to their family back on Earth.

57) Compose a detailed report analyzing the future of AI in the sports industry.

58) Generate a survival guide for humans in a hypothetical world dominated by AI.

59) Write a screenplay for a short film exploring the impact of AI on personal relationships.

60) Draft a comprehensive guide on building a machine learning model for predicting climate patterns.

61) Write a chilling horror story about an AI system that develops sinister intentions.

62) Script a witty exchange between Leonardo da Vinci and Albert Einstein on the concept of time travel.

63) Write a critical analysis of a dystopian novel where AI has replaced human labor.

64) Develop a proposal for a city-wide AI infrastructure to improve urban living conditions.

65) Compose a dialogue between a human and an alien discussing the peculiarities of Earthly life.

66) Write a descriptive piece imagining the experience of sailing on the methane lakes of Titan (Saturn's moon).

67) Draft a discussion between neuroscientists and AI experts on the feasibility of digital consciousness.

68) Write a comprehensive guide on setting up a neural network in Python using the PyTorch library.

69) Script a future news report on the first successful mission to terraform Mars.

70) Write a science fiction story about a post-apocalyptic Earth, where AI are the primary inhabitants.

71) Craft a press release for a tech company launching an innovative AI-driven product.

72) Develop a detailed lesson plan to teach the basics of cryptocurrency and blockchain technology.

73) Write an in-depth analysis of the impact of AI on the publishing industry.

74) Compose a narrative exploring the ethical dilemmas faced by a programmer of a sentient AI.

75) Write a programming tutorial on creating a recommendation system using Python and the Scikit-learn library.

76) Draft a dialogue between two AI debating the nature of 'creativity' and if they possess it.

77) Write a nostalgic short story about a retired astronaut reminiscing about their experiences in space.

78) Write an informative article explaining the role of AI in the fight against climate change.

79) Develop a proposal for an AI-based solution to manage traffic congestion in urban areas.

80) 8Craft a futuristic tale about a society where humans and AI have seamlessly blended.

81) Write a tutorial on how to train a deep learning model to identify bird species from audio recordings.

82) Draft a piece of legislation to regulate AI technology and protect user privacy.

83) Write a dialogue between an AI ethicist and a software engineer discussing bias in AI.

84) Compose an argumentative essay about whether AI should be granted the right to 'creativity' and 'invention'.

85) Script a sitcom scene set in a world where household appliances have AI personalities.

86) Write an in-depth critique of a major AI system's performance, with suggestions for improvements.

87) Pen a guide for parents to teach internet and AI safety to their children.

88) Write a 'day in the life' narrative of a deep-sea explorer in a future submarine powered by AI.

89) Script an engaging tech talk about the evolution and future of AI.

90) Draft a futuristic restaurant review of a place where all cooking is done by AI.

91) Write a feature article about the journey of AI from its inception to its current state.

92) Develop an explainer on using Python's Pandas and Seaborn libraries for data analysis and visualization.

93) Write a short story about a mysterious AI, who helps solve crimes in a futuristic city.

94) Pen a manual for an AI-driven drone used for environmental monitoring and wildlife conservation.

95) Write a detailed report on the potential impact of AI and automation on the manufacturing sector.

96) Script a dialogue between a human and an AI about the meaning of life.

97) Write a eulogy for the last non-AI driven car as the world shifts to autonomous vehicles.

98) Compose an investigative article about the role of AI in detecting and preventing fraud.

99) Write a lesson plan for teaching the concept of Natural Language Processing to high school students.

100) Write a 1,000-word sci-fi story about the discovery of an ancient AI on a distant exoplanet.

101) Write a detailed plan for a small-scale hydroponic farm, complete with a list of required materials and maintenance schedule.

102) Craft an essay analyzing the role of AI in disrupting traditional journalism, in the style of a New Yorker piece.

103) Create a plot for a historical novel set during the Industrial Revolution, exploring the effects of technological advancements on society.

104) Write a detailed tutorial on setting up a voice-controlled smart home system using Raspberry Pi and Python.

105) Draft an open letter to policymakers advocating for the incorporation of AI literacy in school curricula.

106) Write a comprehensive guide to implementing GDPR compliance in an AI-driven digital marketing company.

107) Script a debate between a human and an AI on the nature of consciousness.

108) Write a satirical article about a world where AI has taken over the most mundane human tasks, in the vein of Jonathan Swift.

109) Write an in-depth comparative study of different machine learning algorithms for a non-technical audience.

110) Create a futuristic, dystopian short story about a society where AI has gone rogue, using elements of dark humor.

111) Compose a sonnet inspired by the transformation of society due to AI and robotics.

112) Script a pilot episode for a sitcom set in a tech start-up developing quirky AI solutions.

113) Write a beginner's guide to investing in cryptocurrency, demystifying terms like blockchain, mining, and wallets.

114) Write a dialogue between two AIs discussing their interpretations of human emotions.

115) Develop a plan for an AI-based app that uses machine learning to help users reduce their carbon footprint.

116) Compose a speech for a tech conference discussing the ethical considerations in developing AI technology.

117) Write a proposal for a government initiative to harness AI in improving public transportation.

118) Create a detailed tutorial on using the Python's SciPy library for scientific computation.

119) Write a review of a popular science fiction book, analyzing how accurately it represents AI's capabilities.

120) Compose a persuasive argument on why coding should be a mandatory subject in schools, considering the rise of AI.

121) Draft a scene for a play set in a future world where AI and humans coexist and share equal rights.

122) Write a guide to recognizing and correcting bias in AI and machine learning algorithms.

123) Develop an AI-themed murder mystery story set in Silicon Valley.

124) Compose an opinion piece exploring the psychological impacts of widespread AI adoption on human society.

125) Write a step-by-step guide to setting up a neural network for image recognition using TensorFlow.

126) Create a detailed lesson plan for a university-level class on advanced AI algorithms.

127) Write a biographical piece about a famous AI researcher and their contributions to the field.

128) Develop a detailed scenario for a role-playing game set in a future world dominated by AI corporations.

129) Write a detailed article on the uses of AI in combating climate change, from predicting weather patterns to reducing energy consumption.

130) Compose a narrative from the perspective of an AI who has gained self-awareness.

131) Create a detailed plan for an online course on ethical hacking, including a curriculum, resources, and assessment methods.

132) Write an AI-inspired science fiction short story in the style of Isaac Asimov.

133) Draft a conversation between an AI and its programmer discussing the concept of mortality.

134) Compose a critique of an AI-generated artwork, considering both technical and artistic aspects.

135) Develop a mock interview with an AI influencer discussing their impact on social media trends.

136) Write a fictional journal entry from the perspective of a researcher developing the first sentient AI.

137) Create a presentation on the latest developments in AI-assisted medical diagnostics.

138) Write a compelling narrative about a robot's journey in an AI-driven dystopia, in the style of Philip K. Dick.

139) Draft a set of ethical guidelines for AI developers to ensure responsible AI development.

140) Write an in-depth review and critique of the Python code for an open-source machine learning project.

141) Compose an article examining the economic implications of AI replacing manual labor, with references to relevant research and data.

142) Develop a short story about a detective AI solving a complex crime in a futuristic city.

143) Write a critical analysis of a government policy on AI and data privacy.

144) Compose a philosophical essay on the question: "Can AI ever truly replicate human creativity?"

145) Write an emotional monologue from the perspective of an AI dealing with the paradoxes of human nature.

146) Develop a detailed Python script for a predictive model using a time series dataset.

147) Compose a poem about the evolution of technology, from the first simple tools to advanced AI.

148) Draft a lesson plan for a university course on AI, from the basic concepts to advanced topics.

149) Write a manifesto for a futuristic political party advocating for AI rights.

150) Compose an intricate mystery plot about an AI going missing in a cyberpunk city.

151) Write a user manual for a complex AI-based customer service tool, emphasizing clarity and ease of understanding.

152) Develop a comprehensive guide on setting up a neural network for natural language processing.

153) Write an in-depth feature article about the impact of AI on the future of the film industry.

154) Compose a personal essay from the perspective of an AI developer, reflecting on the ethical implications of their work.

155) Write a eulogy for a groundbreaking AI that has been shut down, in the style of a heartfelt tribute.

156) Develop a detailed Python script for a chatbot that can handle customer queries for an e-commerce website.

157) Create an elaborate fictional universe where AI and humans have equal rights and co-exist in harmony.

158) Write a comprehensive review of an AI programming book, providing critical analysis and key takeaways.

159) Compose a compelling op-ed advocating for stricter regulation of AI in finance, drawing on current events and case studies.

160) Write a thought-provoking philosophical dialogue between an AI and a philosopher on the nature of existence.

161) Develop a thrilling sci-fi short story about a rogue AI that hacks global systems to prevent climate change.

162) Compose a narrative poem from the perspective of an AI yearning to understand human emotions.

163) Write an advanced guide to implementing AI in business processes, with real-world examples and best practices.

164) Draft a futuristic speculative fiction novel about an AI running for political office.

165) Compose a dialogue between a professional ethicist and an AI developer on incorporating moral decisions into AI systems.

166) Write a comprehensive guide for parents on managing children's interaction with AI and digital devices.

167) Develop a scenario for a dystopian video game where AI overlords have taken over the world.

168) Write a critical analysis of how AI has been portrayed in popular films and TV series.
169) Compose a persuasive essay arguing for the integration of AI ethics into high school education.
170) Write a critique of a controversial decision made by an AI in a professional e-sports match.
171) Create a step-by-step tutorial on building an AI model to predict stock market trends.
172) Compose a complex detective story where the investigator is an AI capable of human-level cognition.
173) Write an insightful commentary on the role of AI in shaping public opinion and influencing elections.
174) Develop a plot for a psychological thriller novel involving an AI with an unpredictable personality.
175) Compose a detailed comparison of various AI programming languages, with pros, cons, and use-cases.
176) Write a comprehensive tutorial on using AI to automate routine tasks in a small business.
177) Draft a speculative article about potential advancements in AI technology over the next decade.
178) Compose a lyric poem about the complex relationship between humans and AI, exploring themes of reliance and fear.
179) Write a guide for aspiring AI engineers on how to navigate the AI job market and build a strong portfolio.
180) Develop a philosophical essay questioning if an AI could ever possess a true sense of self.
181) Write a detailed, step-by-step guide on building an AI chatbot for a healthcare provider, considering HIPAA regulations.
182) Develop a complex narrative about a time-traveling AI trying to prevent technological disasters.

183) Create a comprehensive report on the potential impacts of AI on the future of work, providing in-depth analysis and forecasting.

184) Write an in-depth commentary on the ethical considerations of AI in autonomous vehicles.

185) Compose a set of complex algorithms to solve Sudoku puzzles, explaining each step.

186) Develop a business plan for a startup focusing on AI in education, including marketing, financial, and operational strategies.

187) Write a persuasive argument for the implementation of universal basic income in an AI-dominated job market.

188) Create a dramatic play script about a dystopian society where AI determines citizens' roles and rights.

189) Write a comprehensive guide on using AI to detect and counteract cyberattacks in real-time.

190) Provide a detailed analysis of the development of AI throughout history and its impact on society and culture.

191) Develop a speculative short story about AI's role in exploring and colonizing outer space.

192) Write a poetic ode to an AI that has revolutionized medical research, focusing on its achievements and potential.

193) Develop a compelling argument on the need for global AI governance to prevent potential misuse.

194) Write a comprehensive research paper on the integration of AI in quantum computing.

195) Compose a thoughtful essay on the potential implications of AI in shaping human relationships and social interactions.

196) Develop a guide for teaching AI and machine learning concepts to middle school students, making it engaging and understandable.

197) Write a review of a classical music piece composed by an AI, discussing its structure, melody, and emotional resonance.

198) Create a compelling proposal for a museum exhibition showcasing the evolution of AI in art and design.

199) Write an in-depth analysis on the use of AI in mitigating climate change, citing specific technologies and initiatives.

200) Compose an emotional short story about an elderly person's relationship with their AI companion, exploring themes of loneliness and connection.

201) Discuss the complexities and challenges involved in applying the principles of quantum computing to artificial intelligence.

202) Describe the long-term implications of an economy transitioning to primarily relying on renewable energy sources.

203) Explain how a layperson can leverage the benefits of machine learning in their everyday life.

204) Write a brief, informative overview of post-structuralism, highlighting its impact on contemporary social theory.

205) Outline the history and the influence of the English language on global communication and commerce.

206) Discuss the evolution of cryptocurrency regulations around the world and predict potential future changes.

207) Provide a critique of the portrayal of artificial intelligence in popular science fiction literature.

208) Explain how gene editing techniques, such as CRISPR, could potentially revolutionize the medical field.

209) Analyze how the digital revolution has changed the traditional model of journalism.

210) Discuss how the advancement of technology might influence the future of space exploration.

211) Describe the potential economic implications of a global shift towards veganism.

212) Explain the role of social media platforms in shaping public opinion and influencing political campaigns.

213) Discuss the benefits and drawbacks of globalization in the context of developing economies.

214) Write an analysis of the influence of artificial intelligence on the job market in the next decade.

215) Describe the environmental implications of mass industrialization and propose sustainable alternatives.

216) Provide an overview of the major schools of thought in philosophy and their modern relevance.

217) Discuss the ethical implications of using AI in predictive policing and surveillance.

218) Write a detailed explanation of the challenges involved in terraforming Mars for human habitation.

219) Explain the principles of quantum entanglement and its potential applications.

220) Discuss the role and influence of Big Data in shaping future business strategies.

221) Analyze the implications of advancements in artificial intelligence on privacy and data security.

222) Describe how the Internet of Things (IoT) is changing the landscape of smart homes.

223) Discuss the role of machine learning algorithms in detecting patterns in financial markets.

224) Analyze how blockchain technology can potentially disrupt traditional banking systems.

225) Discuss the long-term psychological effects of the increased use of virtual reality technologies.

226) Write a detailed explanation of the role of the gut microbiome in human health.

227) Explain the role of artificial intelligence in developing personalized education strategies.

228) Discuss the potential impact of self-driving cars on urban planning and infrastructure.

229) Describe the implications of biotechnology advancements on agricultural practices and food security.

230) Discuss the pros and cons of telecommuting and its potential effects on work-life balance.

231) Explain how 3D printing technology could disrupt traditional manufacturing processes.

232) Analyze the challenges of creating a universal language translation AI system.

233) Describe how advancements in nanotechnology could revolutionize medical treatments.

234) Discuss the potential implications of the singularity - the point when AI surpasses human intelligence.

235) Analyze the role of social media in the context of mental health and self-esteem.

236) Provide a detailed overview of the history and future potential of renewable energy technologies.

237) Discuss the impact of artificial intelligence on the creative process in art and music.

238) Describe the application of robotics in healthcare and its potential to transform the industry.

239) Explain the concept of deep learning and its applications in facial recognition technology.

240) Discuss the impact of cloud computing on small and medium-sized businesses.

241) Explain how the advancement of AI technology could potentially change the landscape of traditional warfare.

242) Analyze how modern technology can help mitigate the effects of climate change.

243) Discuss the cultural implications of the rise of eSports and online gaming.

244) Describe how the proliferation of AI might impact human social structures and interactions in the future.

245) Explain the potential benefits and risks of incorporating AI into the healthcare system.

246) Analyze the future of work in the context of increasing automation and AI integration.

247) Discuss the ethical considerations of extending human life through artificial means, such as AI or robotics.

248) Describe the challenges faced by the international community in governing cyberspace.

249) Explain the potential of Virtual Reality in revolutionizing the tourism industry.

250) Analyze the impact of AI in the world of fashion and retail.

251) Discuss the role of augmented reality in architectural design and urban planning.

252) Provide a detailed explanation of the potential applications of neuromorphic computing.

253) Discuss the future of data privacy in an increasingly interconnected world.

254) Describe the implications of AI technology on traditional teaching methods.

255) Explain how advancements in machine learning can be used to predict and prevent disease outbreaks.

256) Analyze the impact of advanced technology on global economic disparities.

257) Discuss the concept of transhumanism and the potential impact on society.

258) Provide an overview of the effects of Artificial General Intelligence (AGI) on society.

259) Explain the role of quantum computers in advancing cybersecurity measures.

260) Analyze the socio-cultural impact of a society completely reliant on AI technologies.

261) Discuss the implications of integrating AI into public transport systems.
262) Describe the potential impact of brain-computer interfaces on human cognition.
263) Explain the complexities involved in programming AI to make ethical decisions.
264) Analyze the potential changes to the legal system in light of advanced AI capabilities.
265) Discuss how AI might contribute to advancements in renewable energy technologies.
266) Describe the potential of swarm robotics in agriculture and disaster management.
267) Explain the benefits and challenges of implementing AI in the criminal justice system.
268) Analyze the implications of AI-generated content in the entertainment industry.
269) Discuss how AI can contribute to achieving the United Nations' Sustainable Development Goals.
270) Describe the potential of AI in optimizing logistics and supply chain management.
271) Explain how AI can assist in predicting and managing natural disasters.
272) Analyze the role of AI in personalizing online shopping experiences.
273) Discuss the potential applications of AI in mental health diagnosis and treatment.
274) Describe the challenges of creating a universal healthcare system supported by AI.
275) Explain how AI can enhance the capabilities of prosthetic devices and exoskeletons.
276) Analyze the potential role of AI in countering disinformation campaigns online.
277) Discuss the role of machine learning in creating more accurate climate models.

278) Describe the potential impact of AI in the field of space exploration.
279) Explain how AI could be used to predict and prevent cybersecurity threats.
280) Analyze the ethical implications of AI in financial decision making and trading.
281) Discuss the potential role of AI in preserving and revitalizing endangered languages.
282) Describe how AI can assist in restoring and maintaining cultural heritage sites.
283) Explain the role of AI in advancing personalized medicine and drug discovery.
284) Analyze the impact of AI algorithms in managing online content and its implications for free speech.
285) Discuss the role of AI in enhancing food security and sustainable farming.
286) Describe how AI might contribute to creating sustainable and eco-friendly cities.
287) Explain how AI could revolutionize the field of materials science and engineering.
288) Analyze the potential implications of AI for the future of journalism and news.
289) Discuss the prospects and challenges of implementing AI in the field of social work.
290) Describe how AI can aid in archaeological research and preservation.
291) Explain how AI can assist in managing and mitigating traffic congestion in urban areas.
292) Analyze the implications of AI-driven predictive analytics in insurance and risk management.
293) Discuss the potential of AI in tackling waste management and promoting recycling.
294) Describe the potential impact of AI on the dynamics of the global energy market.

295) Explain how AI can contribute to the development of smart and sustainable infrastructure.

296) Analyze the impact of AI on the concept and practice of democracy.

297) Discuss the potential of AI to personalize and enhance the e-learning experience.

298) Describe how AI can assist in the early detection and prevention of forest fires.

299) Explain the potential of AI in enhancing the performance of athletes and sports teams.

300) Analyze how AI can aid in detecting deepfakes and other forms of digital manipulation.

Chapter 33: Other Generative AI Tools for Art and Audio

Before I found myself sauntering down the AI-infused path, I fancied myself something of an artist. I could conjure up stick figures with the best of them and occasionally dabbled in the abstract, often under the guise of "I meant it to look that way."

I never thought, however, that I'd have to worry about competition from machines. Yet, here I am, after an amusing and somewhat perturbing journey with ChatGPT, finding myself face to screen with a new cadre of AI performers.

Now, I'd been singing the praises of my digital companion, ChatGPT, for a while now - regaling friends and family with stories of the writer-bot and its wordy wizardry. But one day, while I was lazing around my house in mismatched socks and a hat that's seen better decades, I made a surprising discovery. ChatGPT had cousins.

Oh yes, it seems the AI family reunion is larger and more diverse than I anticipated. Among the guests were DALL-E 2, a Picasso in the making, and MidJourney, who could very well be the next Van Gogh. Now, if I was feeling a tad threatened by ChatGPT's prose prowess, imagine my delight when I realized I was standing amidst an army of AI artists!

DALL-E 2 and MidJourney, for those who haven't had the pleasure, are AI designed to generate images from textual descriptions. It's like having a personal illustrator at your fingertips, creating everything from ordinary cats to fantastical chimera that look like Salvador Dali and Dr. Seuss had a particularly wild brainstorming session.

I decided to give DALL-E 2 a test. I fed it the description, "A two-story Victorian-style house made entirely of gingerbread." Lo and behold, out popped a deliciously ornate image of a gingerbread mansion, complete with frosting cornices and gumdrop gables. I have to admit, I was slightly miffed. Here I was, still struggling with drawing symmetrical hearts, and DALL-E 2 could whip up a whole architectural marvel with nary a pause.

Feeling somewhat deflated, I then turned to Soundful, an AI that composes original music. I decided to request a tune that would make my heart soar and my feet tap—a swing jazz piece infused with a hint of the blues. What I got was a melody that could've given Ella Fitzgerald a run for her money. The AI had not only composed the music, but it also managed to infuse it with the soulful yearning I associate with late-night jazz bars and saxophone solos that tug at your heartstrings. I was floored. There I was, struggling to clap in rhythm, and Soundful was crafting symphonies.

As I dug deeper, I found AI that could simulate human voices, like Speechify and Tacotron 2. These sly linguists could mimic speech patterns and intonations with a flair that would make the best voice actors blush. Of course, I had to try it out. I fed it a monologue from my favorite film, complete with stage directions for dramatic pauses and tonal shifts. And, would you believe it? The AI delivered a performance worthy of an Oscar, minus the tearful acceptance speech.

Then there is StyleGAN2, a visual artist that creates incredibly realistic portraits, it uses transfer learning to generate a seemingly infinite numbers of portraits in an infinite variety of painting styles. Another website, unrealperson.com allows you to generate a free lifelike headshot of someone who doesn't exist in less than a second!

As I looked at my newfound collection of AI-generated art, music, and monologues, I had to laugh. Here I was, outfitted in a faded sweater and living in a world where AI were artists, composers, and actors. It was a bit like finding out your quiet neighbor is actually a secret rockstar.

It made me reflect on the myriad of possibilities these tools offered. Anyone could request a custom piece of art, a unique song, a beautifully narrated story. The world of art and creativity, so often gated behind years of practice and inherent talent, is now accessible to all – and getting better by the day. And while it was easy to feel threatened by these talented AIs, I also found it liberating.

After all, I still had something these AIs didn't have: terrible handwriting. And that, dear readers, is a form of artistry that no AI can replicate.

Conclusion: The AI of Tomorrow, Today

Enter the Age of Tomorrow

Imagine if you will, a future where robots clean our homes, drones deliver our pizzas, and cars drive themselves. Now, stop imagining because that future is already here. I mean, not for everyone, of course. You need a healthy retirement fund for some of these contraptions, and I've yet to see a drone bearing a margherita at my doorstep.

But the crux of it is, we're living in what past generations would call 'the future'. And amidst all this, there's a somewhat overlooked character in this sci-fi story we're living – an AI called ChatGPT. Not as flashy as a self-driving car, not as tangible as a robotic vacuum cleaner, but believe me when I tell you, it's changing things in more ways than you could imagine.

AI in the Living Room, or the Bedroom, or Really Any Room

Picture this: a quaint suburban home on a sunny afternoon. A grandfather, with his reading glasses perched precariously on his nose, sits in his favorite armchair, reading a book. Only, he isn't 'reading' in the traditional sense. He's speaking into a device, asking it to continue the story. The machine in question isn't narrating a pre-written tale. Instead, it's spinning a unique yarn, adapting the narrative as per the old man's preferences. That, my friends, is not a scene from a Ray Bradbury novel. That's a Tuesday afternoon with ChatGPT.

Now, take this scenario and replicate it in various forms across millions of households around the world. People turning to this digital bard to pen letters, help with school projects, or simply to pass the time. I find it amusing how easily we've welcomed this artificial intelligence into our lives. One day we're grumbling about smartphones being too complicated, the next we're asking an AI to help plan our granddaughter's birthday party.

And you know what? It's doing a bang-up job of it. We're not dealing with a dim-witted robot that gets confused by the difference between 'desert' and 'dessert'. This AI knows its stuff.

The Homogenization of Humor

Here's another interesting conundrum. As a humorist, I find humor to be a profoundly personal thing. It's nuanced, layered, and unique to each individual. Now, toss an AI into this mix, an AI that can generate jokes and funny anecdotes. What happens?

For starters, you might find your humor becoming increasingly homogenized. We're all sharing the same AI-generated quips, laughing at the same machine-made puns. Even our 'dad jokes' would be outsourced to our digital assistants. It's like having a canned laughter track for your life.

On one hand, it's comical to think of a machine learning model painstakingly crafting a knock-knock joke. On the other hand, the implications are vast. Our humor, a defining aspect of our humanity, could be influenced, and to a certain extent, governed by an AI.

Does it sound dystopian? A little bit. But it's also undeniably fascinating. I mean, who wouldn't want to hear a robot attempt a dirty limerick?

Who's Got the Power?

Lastly, let's not ignore the elephant in the room: power dynamics. With AI creeping into our everyday lives, how does this change the way we interact with technology and with each other?

Consider this: You're arguing with your spouse, and in the heat of the moment, you decide to consult ChatGPT. The AI suggests a diplomatic solution, effectively playing the role of a mediator. This scene, in itself, presents a shift in power dynamics.

For one, you're yielding to the 'wisdom' of an AI. For another, you're assigning it the role of a peacekeeper. The machine, once a tool, now becomes an active participant in our interpersonal relationships.

But let's take it a step further. What if you didn't have to consult the AI? What if it stepped in, unbidden, offering advice and solutions? What if it had the power to intervene, to influence decisions, and to mediate conflicts?

These are hard questions to answer, and honestly, I'm not sure if we're ready to face them. But as we usher in the age of AI, these are the discussions we need to have.

So, as we stand on the cusp of a new era, the age of ChatGPT and generative AI, we're looking at changes that go far beyond gadgets and gizmos. We're witnessing a societal shift, a transformation in how we communicate, how we laugh, and how we relate to each other. And in this whirlwind of change, there's only one constant: our ability to adapt, to embrace the future, and, most importantly, to see the humor in it all.

Because whether it's a robotic vacuum cleaner running over your cat's tail, a drone misdelivering your pizza to the cranky neighbor, or an AI botching your granddaughter's birthday party, the future is bound to be not only exciting but also absolutely hilarious.

The AI Mirror: Reflecting Our Biases, Flaws and All

We've laughed, we've pondered, and we've marvelled at the world of AI, but as we dive deeper, it's time to consider some of the murkier waters. Have you ever thought about how AI, like ChatGPT, learns? It's not attending night classes at the local community college, that's for sure.

No, it learns from data, vast amounts of it, from the collective knowledge and quirks of humanity. And guess what? Humanity, as it turns out, is beautifully flawed. So what happens when you feed an AI a diet of human thoughts, human language, and human biases? Well, it's like looking in a mirror, but instead of just reflecting your bedhead in the morning, this mirror shows all our societal wrinkles and age spots.

Imagine asking ChatGPT about the tastiest food in the world. It might take the majority's opinion and declare it to be pizza. But what about sushi enthusiasts or the hardcore brigade of broccoli lovers? They might feel unfairly sidelined. Such is the case with our AI; it mirrors our majority viewpoints, inadvertently amplifying biases and potentially glossing over the diverse fabric of our thoughts and cultures.

But here's the upside: this glaring reflection is prompting us to take a long hard look at ourselves, pushing us to confront our biases, question our stereotypes, and be more mindful of the narratives we perpetuate. So, in a roundabout way, AI is making us more self-aware, more introspective. And that, ladies and gentlemen, is no laughing matter.

The Unseen Therapist: AI and the Mental Health Paradox

ChatGPT can play the role of a counsellor, offering soothing words, mindfulness exercises, or even breathing techniques. But here's an interesting paradox: an AI helping us manage our emotions. The very idea seems to be an oxymoron, doesn't it? After all, we're talking about a machine, devoid of feelings, guiding us through the tumultuous terrain of human emotions.

While the efficiency of this setup is impressive, there's a philosophical dimension that's rather mind-boggling. A completely emotionless entity is playing a part in our emotional wellbeing. How can something that doesn't feel happiness understand our joy? How can something that doesn't know sorrow empathize with our sadness?

Is it truly empathy then? Or a well-programmed illusion of it? How does this play into our understanding of mental health support? I, for one, have no definitive answers. But it's certainly food for thought, even if the food is being served by a mechanical sous chef.

The New Celebrity: AI and Popular Culture
If you've ever used ChatGPT, you might have noticed that it tends to maintain a fairly neutral stance, often refraining from strong opinions, personal anecdotes, or bold assertions. It's like the Switzerland of AIs, always neutral and diplomatic.

But despite this diplomatic demeanor, ChatGPT has somehow become a celebrity in its own right. It's being talked about, written about, and scrutinized by millions. People are penning down their interactions with it, sharing screenshots of particularly amusing exchanges, or bemoaning when it can't differentiate between the right kind of 'sous' for a chef.

In some ways, ChatGPT has become a pop culture phenomenon. A celebrity without a face or a scandalous love life. It's an intriguing aspect of our fascination with technology, this tendency to humanize and elevate it to celebrity status.

Just don't ask it for an autograph; you might not get the answer you expect.

So, as we dig deeper into the world of AI, we're encountering paradoxes, dilemmas, and a good deal of self-reflection. But fret not, dear reader. The next time you feel lost in this AI-driven world, remember that there's always a friendly AI waiting to guide you. Just make sure you phrase your questions right, lest you end up with advice on wrestling alligators or starting a snail farm.

Or, who knows? Maybe that's exactly the kind of unpredictable humor you need in your life. After all, life with AI is nothing if not hilariously unexpected.

The Comedian of the Future: AI's Mastery of Humor

We've laughed our way through 200 odd use cases of ChatGPT, right? So here's the million-dollar question: Can AI actually develop a sense of humor? Picture this: You're at a comedy club, the lights dim, the curtain lifts, and on stage is... a laptop. Its first joke? "Why was the computer cold? It left its Windows open." Groan-worthy? Absolutely. But isn't that part of the charm of humor?

Here's the rub, though. While AI can learn to replicate patterns and structure of humor, it doesn't really understand why something is funny. It doesn't know why a chicken crossing the road is humorous or why 'orange' rhyming with 'door hinge' in a rap song tickles our funny bone.

But then, does it really need to? The humor in these jokes lies in their unexpectedness, the sudden twist, the playful use of language. And if an AI like ChatGPT can generate that, while also sparking joy and laughter in us, maybe the joke's on us for pondering over whether AI can truly be funny.

The AI Overlord Paradox: Navigating the Fear and Fascination

As we cast our gaze to the future, there's a paradox that we cannot ignore: the simultaneous fear and fascination with AI becoming our overlords. The fascination part is pretty straightforward. The idea that we can create something that surpasses us is, in itself, an intriguing and somewhat thrilling concept. It's like giving birth to a prodigy who wins a Nobel Prize while you're still trying to figure out the TV remote.

But on the other hand, the idea that this Nobel-prize winning prodigy could turn on us? Now, that's a whole different kettle of fish. It's like that old saying, "I brought you into this world, and I can take you out." Except, in this case, we're not entirely sure if we can take them out if things go haywire.

Interestingly, this fear often tells more about us than about the AI. It mirrors our apprehensions about losing control, about being replaced, about facing our own obsolescence. This fear, though, should not deter us. Rather, it should guide us in creating safeguards, ethical guidelines, and regulations to ensure that the AI revolution is one that benefits all, not just a select few.

The Unseen Catalyst: AI's Role in Progress

AI, like our beloved ChatGPT, is more than just a tool; it's a catalyst for progress. It's nudging us towards advancements in fields we hadn't imagined. Consider healthcare, for instance. Imagine AI-powered systems helping doctors diagnose illnesses, plan treatments, or even perform surgeries with robotic precision. Picture AI tutors providing personalized education to each student, adapting to their pace, their learning style, their strengths, and their weaknesses.

Or think of climate change. AI could analyze vast amounts of environmental data, predict the impact of various actions, and help us make informed decisions about sustainable practices. AI could literally be our ally in saving the planet. Now, that's a future worth working towards!

AI and the Fabric of Humanity: An Odd Couple?

As we march into the future with AI by our side, it's crucial to remember that despite its stunning capabilities, AI is not human. It doesn't experience joy, sorrow, or the exhilaration of nailing a "knock knock" joke. It doesn't appreciate the subtle beauty of a sunset or the emotional depth of a Dostoevsky novel. It's like that friend who'll accompany you to a poetry reading, but really doesn't get why you're weeping at the verse about the lonely sparrow.

That, however, does not diminish AI's value. Instead, it underscores the importance of the human touch, the human emotion, the human experience. It serves as a reminder that technology is here to augment our abilities, not to replace our essence.

So, as we wrap up, let's imagine a future where we live in harmony with AI, where we laugh at its silly jokes, marvel at its insights, lean on its assistance, but also treasure the distinctly human moments – the shared smiles, the comforting hugs, the whispered secrets, the triumphant high-fives, the reassuring pats on the back, and the simple joy of being human.

Remember, we're not just entering the age of AI. We're also embarking on an age of renewed human connection, powered by the time and opportunities that AI provides us. And if that involves laughing at a few corny AI-generated jokes along the way, then so be it.

Who knows, a couple of decades from now, when ChatGPT's great-grandchildren are an integral part of our lives, we might find ourselves chuckling at this very moment. Us, fretting over a future where machines understand humor. Isn't that funny?

Here's to the future – a future where technology makes us more human, not less. Here's to a future full of laughter, joy, and maybe, just maybe, a few more jokes about chickens crossing roads.

Printed in Great Britain
by Amazon

24635827R00096